Chicken
Cookbook
by Jean Wickstrom
Foods Editor, *Southern Living* Magazine

Library of Congress Catalog Card Number: 75-32258

ISBN 0-8487-0409-6

Manufactured in the United States of America

Third Printing 1982

Chicken Cookbook

Editor: Martha Fazio
Cover Photograph: Gerald Crawford
Illustrations: John Anderson
Cover Recipe: Chicken Pie Superb

Contents

Introduction

Chicken is one dish you can count on to be a favorite with family and guests. Its popularity is quite understandable since chicken can come to the table in an endless variety of dishes: as a dinner entrée, luncheon dish, or even as a tempting appetizer. Chicken is also a popular choice for picnics, cookouts, and barbecues.

Thanks to its delicate flavor, chicken takes naturally to many seasonings and cooking methods. Since it teams well with fruits and vegetables, it can be dressed up for company occasions without extravagant expenditures of time or money. Such versatility makes chicken one of the best food buys.

This book features recipes for chicken prepared in a variety of ways. Thus, you'll enjoy many new and unusual chicken dishes plus all-time Southern favorites. Moreover, you'll find dishes suitable for any occasion in this assortment of over 300 delicious chicken recipes.

In addition to the recipes, the information on the buying and storing of chicken will prove helpful. The instructions and illustrations for cutting up a whole chicken, boning a chicken breast, and carving a roast chicken are also important lessons in chicken cookery. Perfect these techniques and all the many facets of chicken cookery are open to you.

The adaptability of chicken is limitless—from picnic to party, from country to cosmopolitan—but no matter how you cook it, chicken is always a winner.

All About Chicken

As its past and present popularity proves, chicken is a delicious and versatile meat; at the same time, chicken is nutritious and economical. Once you have learned of its potential by examining the multitude of recipes gathered here, you will want to take advantage of grocery specials on chicken and always have some close at hand in your freezer. To help you in selecting the type of chicken that will best suit your family's needs, this chapter contains information about buying and storing chicken as well as an explanation of its nutritive value.

Some of the recipes in this book require chicken pieces, others require chicken breasts or boned chicken breasts; still others instruct that the chicken be cooked whole and then carved. Your butcher can perform these operations for you, but his expertise is expensive, and it is rarely convenient to take a whole chicken from the freezer, thaw it, and then trundle off to have someone cut it up. The solution is to learn to carry out these three cutting techniques yourself. Just follow the step-by-step instructions and illustrations in this chapter, and you'll soon be cutting up chickens, boning breasts, and carving well-cooked entrées with aplomb.

Selecting and buying chicken

At the supermarket poultry is sold under several different labels. This list explains the different types of chicken and the labels under which it can be purchased in the supermarket.

Broiler-Fryer: This is an all-purpose chicken that is marketed at 7 to 9 weeks of age and ranges in weight from 2 to 3½ pounds. It may be labeled in the meat counter as a broiling chicken, fryer, or roasting chicken.

Roaster: The roaster is larger and older than the broiler-fryer. It weighs 3½ to 5 pounds and is marketed at 12 to 16 weeks of age.

Hen or Stewing Chicken: This is a plump, meaty, and less tender chicken weighing about 4½ to 6 pounds. A mature hen is usually marketed when 1½ years old. It is best cooked by simmering and is used in soups, stews, salads, and casseroles.

Capon: This is a large bird weighing about 4 to 7 pounds. Excellent for roasting, the capon has a fine flavor and a generous amount of white meat.

Cornish Game Hen: This is a young chicken, usually marketed at 4 to 6 weeks of age, weighing about 1 to 1½ pounds. A Cornish hen is usually sold frozen and is ideal for stuffing and then roasting. Plan one small hen for an individual serving.

Chicken can be purchased in a variety of styles—from whole chicken to boned chicken breasts, from packages of dark meat to packages of white meat. Select the style of chicken that best suits your cooking purpose and your family's preference. These are some of the choices:

Whole Chicken: Giblets are often packed inside body cavity. The meat yield for a whole chicken is about 50 percent of purchased weight. Allow ½ to ¾ pound per serving.

Chicken Halves: These are whole chickens that are split down the center. Ideal for baking, broiling, and grilling. Allow one chicken half per serving.

Chicken Quarters: A chicken quarter may be breast with wing attached or drumstick with thigh attached. Ideal for broiling, baking, and grilling. Allow at least one quarter per serving.

Chicken Pieces: A whole chicken cut in 8 or 9 pieces. Package includes drumsticks, breasts, thighs, wings, and possibly a back.

Breasts: These are the meatiest part of the chicken and can be purchased whole or split. They are all white meat and usually weigh 12 to 15 ounces each. Allow ½ breast per serving. Boned breasts are 100 percent edible meat and are frequently labeled "chicken cutlets."

Thighs: These are meaty portions of dark meat, each weighing about 4 ounces. Allow 2 thighs per serving.

Drumsticks: These dark meat pieces weigh about 4 ounces each. Allow 2 drumsticks per serving.

Wings: This white meat makes ideal hors d'oeuvres. Each wing weighs about 2 ounces. Allow 3 wings per serving.

Giblets: The gizzard, liver, and heart are 100 percent edible. Allow ¼ pound per serving.

Care in handling and storing chicken

Care in handling and storing this perishable product is very important. Properly wrapped, fresh chicken may be kept in the coldest part of the refrigerator for two days. To keep it longer, separate chicken into portions desired, rewrap and label the chicken, and freeze immediately.

Freezing Chicken: Cooked or uncooked chicken freezes well. Use moisture-vaporproof packaging to keep the chicken from drying out or developing "freezer burn." Packaging of this type includes heavy-duty aluminum foil, freezer paper, or heavy plastic bags. Rigid freezer containers with tightly fitting lids are useful when packing cooked chicken dishes containing sauces or other liquids. Do not stuff whole chickens before freezing.

The maximum freezer storage time for chicken which has been wrapped and stored under the most favorable conditions is 6 months for uncooked chicken and 3 months for cooked chicken dishes.

Thawing Chicken: It is best to thaw the chicken with the wrapping loosened in the refrigerator. To thaw a whole chicken (about 4 pounds), allow 12 to 16 hours in the refrigerator. Chicken pieces require about 4 to 9 hours in the refrigerator.

To quick-thaw, place chicken in bag in cold water. With this method, a whole chicken will be pliable in 1 to 3 hours.

Once chicken has been thawed, it is unwise to refreeze cooked or uncooked chicken.

Nutritive value of chicken

Chicken is recognized by nutritionists as an important source of protein, and it is protein of the best quality: rich in essential amino acids which are needed to build and maintain the body's muscles, tissues, and cells.

Moreover, no meat is lower in fat content than chicken—a 3-ounce serving of a skinless broiled chicken breast has only 115 calories—thus it is an important meat for people who must count calories. If chicken is fried or if a sauce is added in preparation, however, the calories will be increased.

Because chicken is a short-fibered meat, it is easy to digest. This is an important consideration when you are selecting food for children, older people, or those who have digestive problems, and it provides another reason for the popularity of chicken.

Timetable for Rotisserie Chicken

Weight	Approximate Total Time
1½ to 2 pounds	¾ to 1¼ hours
2 to 2½ pounds	1¼ to 1½ hours
2½ to 3 pounds	1½ to 1¾ hours

Cutting up a whole chicken

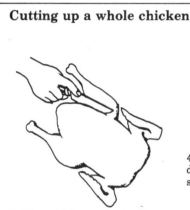

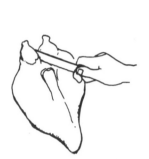

1. Place chicken on its back on cutting board. Using a sharp knife, cut skin between thighs and body of chicken.

4. Find joint between thigh and drumstick. Cut through joint to separate thigh and drumstick.

7. Place the breast, skin side down, on cutting board. Cut through white cartilage at V of neck.

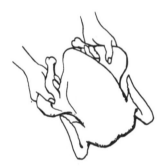

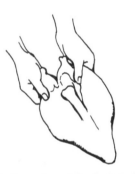

2. Grasping one leg with each hand, lift chicken and bend legs back until bones break at hip joints.

5. Remove wing from body by cutting on inside of wing just over the joint. Cut down and around the joint. To make the wing lie flat, either cut off the wingtip or make a small cut on the inside of the large wing joint. Cut just deep enough to expose the bones.

8. Grasp breast firmly in both hands. Bend back both sides of the breast, and push up with fingers to snap out the breastbone. Cut breast in half lengthwise.

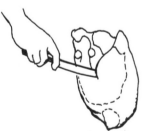

3. To remove leg and thigh from body of chicken, cut from tail to shoulder as closely as possible to the backbone.

6. Separate breast and back by placing the chicken on its neck end and cutting from the tail along each side of backbone through rib joints to neck. Cut through skin that attaches the neck-and-back strip to the breast. Place neck-and-back strip, skin side up, on cutting board. Cut strip into 2 pieces just above the spoon-shaped bones in the back.

Note: When you are handling raw chicken, be sure to thoroughly scrub work surface, utensils, and hands before continuing other food preparation. Scrub cutting boards with cleanser; then rinse and dry well. Avoid putting cooked food on a platter that has contained raw meat without washing the platter.

Timetable for Roasting Chicken*

Weight	Temperature	Time Per Pound	Approximate Total Time
1¹/₂ to 2 pounds	400°	35 to 40 minutes	³/₄ to 1 hour
2 to 2¹/₂ pounds	400°	30 to 35 minutes	1 to 1¹/₄ hours
2¹/₂ to 3 pounds	375°	30 minutes	1¹/₄ to 1¹/₂ hours
3 to 4 pounds	375°	30 minutes	1¹/₂ to 2 hours
5 pounds	375°	30 minutes	About 2¹/₂ hours

*Increase roasting time by 15 minutes when chicken is stuffed.

Boning a chicken breast half

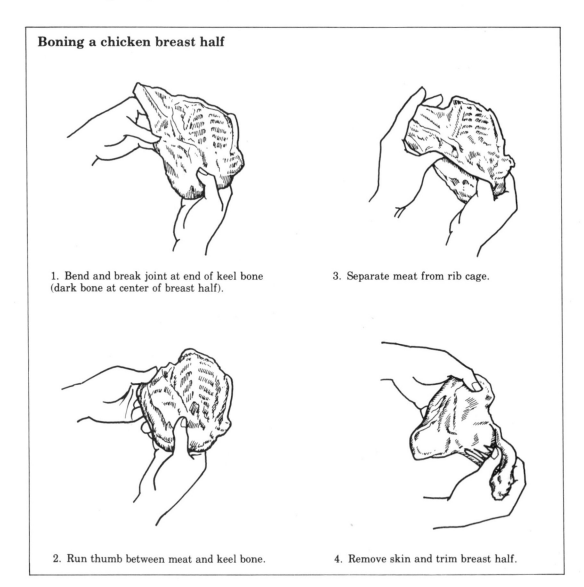

1. Bend and break joint at end of keel bone (dark bone at center of breast half).

3. Separate meat from rib cage.

2. Run thumb between meat and keel bone.

4. Remove skin and trim breast half.

Carving a roast chicken

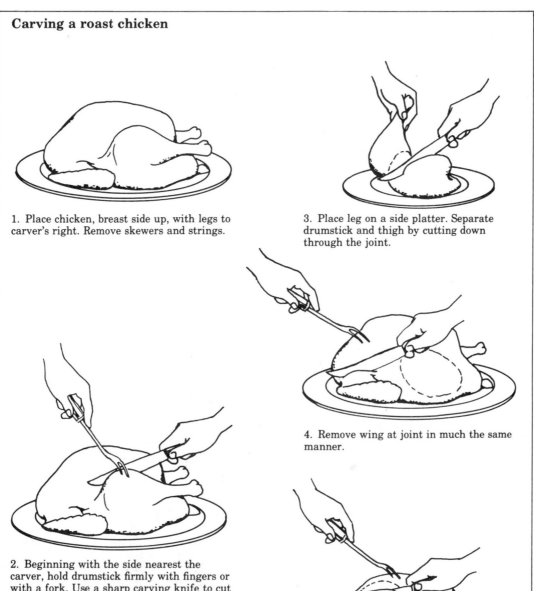

1. Place chicken, breast side up, with legs to carver's right. Remove skewers and strings.

2. Beginning with the side nearest the carver, hold drumstick firmly with fingers or with a fork. Use a sharp carving knife to cut through skin between leg and body. Press against the body of the bird with the flat part of the blade and bend drumstick toward you. Use knife to cut skin and flesh from underside of bird, if necessary.

3. Place leg on a side platter. Separate drumstick and thigh by cutting down through the joint.

4. Remove wing at joint in much the same manner.

5. Insert fork across breastbone. Starting halfway up the breast, carve long, even slices of white meat down to the cut made parallel to the wing. To carve other side of chicken, turn the platter and repeat.

Appetizers

LUAU BITS

10 water chestnuts, cut into halves
 5 chicken livers, cut into quarters
10 slices bacon, cut into halves
 ¼ cup soy sauce
 2 tablespoons firmly packed brown
    sugar

Wrap water chestnuts and chicken livers
in bacon slices. Secure bacon slices with
wooden picks. Marinate in mixture of soy
sauce and brown sugar for 4 hours. Broil
about 3 inches from source of heat until
bacon is crisp. Yield: about 1½ dozen.

CHICKEN LIVER PÂTÉ

1 pound chicken livers
4 hard-cooked eggs
2 medium onions, grated
2 teaspoons salt
¼ teaspoon pepper
2 tablespoons lemon juice
½ cup butter or margarine, melted
   Crackers

Cook chicken livers for 5 minutes in a
small amount of boiling water. Drain.
Combine with hard-cooked eggs, grated
onion, salt, pepper, and lemon juice.
Finely chop, or put in a blender and mix
until smooth. Add melted butter and mix
well. Chill at least 2 to 3 hours. Serve
with crackers. Yield: about 3 cups.

CHICKEN PUFFS

1 (10-ounce) package frozen patty
   shells, thawed
1 (4¾-ounce) can chicken spread
1 tablespoon instant minced onion
1 tablespoon lemon juice
2 tablespoons commercial sour cream
3 tablespoons grated Parmesan
   cheese

Roll each patty shell into a 3-inch square
on a floured board. With a sharp knife,
cut each square in half diagonally. Place
triangles on a cookie sheet. Bake at 400°
for 10 minutes or until golden brown.
Combine chicken spread, onion, lemon
juice, sour cream, and cheese. Split each
triangle horizontally and fill with
chicken mixture. Return to oven for 2
minutes. Serve hot. Yield: 1 dozen.

CHICKEN WITH LEMON AND MUSTARD

3 whole broiler-fryer chicken
   breasts
3 tablespoons butter or margarine
1 tablespoon all-purpose flour
¾ teaspoon Ac'cent
¼ teaspoon salt
1 teaspoon dried leaf tarragon
1 chicken bouillon cube
½ cup hot water
1 tablespoon Dijon mustard
3 thin lemon slices, halved
1 teaspoon finely chopped parsley

Bone chicken breasts; remove skin, and
cut breasts in half. Cut each half into 6
to 8 bite-size squares.
   Melt butter in a large skillet over high
heat. Add chicken; sprinkle with flour,
Ac'cent, salt, and tarragon. Cook 5
minutes, stirring constantly.
   Dissolve bouillon cube in hot water;
add to chicken along with mustard and
lemon slices, stirring to loosen any
browned particles. Cover and cook 2 or 3
minutes. Sprinkle with chopped parsley.
Serve with wooden picks. Yield: 24
servings.

CHICKEN TEMPTERS

8 slices soft white bread
　Softened butter or margarine
1 (4¾-ounce) can chicken spread
¼ cup minced celery
½ to ¾ teaspoon dried basil
　Pimiento strips

Remove crusts from bread and flatten bread with rolling pin. Lightly butter both sides of bread. Bring two diagonally opposite corners of each piece of bread together and secure with a wooden piek. Bake on an ungreased cookie sheet at 400° for 7 to 8 minutes. Remove picks and cool on a wire rack about 30 minutes. Combine chicken spread, celery, and basil; fill bread. Garnish with pimiento strips. Yield: 8 sandwiches.

EASY CHICKEN LIVER PÂTÉ

1 pound chicken livers
½ cup sherry
½ cup melted butter
　Salt, pepper, rosemary, and thyme
　　to taste

Put chicken livers in a saucepan and add sherry to just cover the livers. Simmer over low heat until done, but not tough. Put in blender; add butter and seasonings. Blend and pour into ramekins for serving. Yield: about 3 cups.

CHICKEN-STUFFED CELERY

1 (3-ounce) package cream cheese,
　　softened
1 (4¾-ounce) can chicken spread
½ teaspoon curry powder
24 (1½- to 2-inch) celery slices
　Paprika

Combine cream cheese, chicken spread, and curry. Stuff celery slices. Sprinkle with paprika. Chill. Serve cold. Yield: 24 servings.

SNACK KABOBS

4 slices bacon, quartered
1 (7-ounce) package frozen small
　　crab puffs, partially thawed
1 whole cooked chicken breast,
　　boned and cut into chunks
1 avocado, cut into chunks
16 pineapple chunks
2 bananas, cut into thick slices
　Commercial Italian salad dressing

String meat on short skewers alternately with fruit. Brush with salad dressing. Grill over hot coals, turning once and basting with dressing. Yield: 16 kabobs.

CHERRY-SAUCED CHICKEN WINGS

3 pounds chicken wings
1 (16-ounce) can pitted dark sweet
　　cherries
¼ cup firmly packed brown sugar
2 teaspoons grated fresh gingerroot,
　　or ½ teaspoon ground ginger
1 small clove garlic,
　　minced
½ cup soy sauce
¼ cup port
2 tablespoons lemon juice

Cut off and discard the small wing tips of chicken wings. Cut between the main and second wing joints to make 2 pieces from each wing. Place chicken in a bowl. Place cherries with syrup in a blender and blend until smooth. Add remaining ingredients. Pour over chicken wings and marinate 2 to 3 hours, turning occasionally. Drain, reserving marinade. Place chicken wings in a single layer in baking dish. Bake at 450° for 10 minutes. Reduce temperature to 350°.

Continue to bake 20 minutes longer or until tender, brushing 2 or 3 times with reserved cherry marinade. Serve warm. Yield: about 3 dozen.

Note: Remaining marinade may be thickened with 2 tablespoons cornstarch to serve as a dipping sauce.

COCKTAIL CHICKEN LIVERS WITH GINGER

1 pound chicken livers
¼ cup melted butter
   Salt and freshly ground pepper
   Ground ginger

Cut livers in half; sauté in butter in large skillet over medium heat. Brown livers lightly and evenly; if necessary, use a pair of tongs to turn the individual pieces. (A fork will pierce the livers, causing vital juices to escape.) Do not crowd livers; sauté in batches or use two skillets.

When livers are barely done, a trace of pink may remain; season with salt and pepper and transfer with pan juices to a chafing dish. Serve with wooden picks; guests may dip livers into ginger. Yield: about 30 servings.

CHICKEN WING STICKS

3 pounds chicken wings
½ cup all-purpose flour
½ cup grated Parmesan cheese
1 teaspoon Ac'cent
1 teaspoon salt
1 teaspoon paprika
⅛ teaspoon pepper
½ teaspoon ground oregano
¾ cup buttermilk
   Oil for frying

Cut chicken wings so that you have a drumstick and wingtip. Discard the wingtip, or cook for broth, or reserve for some other use. Blend together dry ingredients in shallow dish. Dip chicken pieces in buttermilk; shake to remove excess. Roll in dry ingredients. Heat oil to 365° and fry chicken for 5 minutes. Drain on absorbent paper. Keep warm in chafing dish. Yield: about 18 servings.

ORANGE CHICKEN FLUFFS

2 (4¾-ounce) cans chicken spread
2 tablespoons chopped toasted
   almonds
¾ cup chopped mandarin oranges
½ cup whipping cream,
   whipped
15 to 20 medium cream puff shells or
   30 to 40 small shells
   Mandarin orange slices

Combine chicken spread, almonds, and chopped oranges; fold in whipped cream. Chill. Fill puff shells with mixture. Garnish top of each with a mandarin orange slice. Yield: 15 to 20 servings.

SHERRIED CHICKEN LIVER PÂTÉ

1 pound chicken livers
   All-purpose flour seasoned with salt
   and pepper
2 tablespoons butter or margarine
1 medium onion, finely chopped
4 tablespoons dry sherry, divided
   Pinch rosemary
   Pinch thyme
6 tablespoons softened butter or
   margarine
2 tablespoons Cognac
   Salt, pepper, and seasoned salt to
   taste
   Parsley sprigs
   Melba rounds

Pat livers dry with paper towels. Sprinkle lightly with seasoned flour. Heat butter in a skillet and sauté livers over medium heat for about 5 minutes. Add onion and continue cooking and stirring until onion is barely yellow, about 3 minutes. Stir in 2 tablespoons sherry, rosemary, and thyme and simmer for a minute. Add softened butter; remove from heat and puree in electric blender, blending ⅓ of the mixture at a time and pushing down from sides into path of blades. When all has been blended until smooth, stir in remaining 2 tablespoons sherry, Cognac, salt, pepper, and seasoned salt to taste. Chill in container from which pâté is to be served. Garnish with clusters of fresh parsley and serve with melba rounds. Yield: about 2½ cups.

CHICKEN WINGS

2 pounds chicken wings
½ cup catsup
¼ cup soy sauce
¼ cup honey
¼ cup lemon juice

Separate chicken wings into 3 pieces. Put the tips aside to use for soup. Marinate the remaining pieces for 3 hours in the mixture made by combining catsup, soy sauce, honey, and lemon juice. Place wings on an aluminum foil covered cookie sheet, making sure that wings do not touch. Bake at 275° for 45 minutes to 1 hour. Yield: about 12 to 14 servings.

GATEAU DE FOIES DE POULARDE

10 to 12 chicken livers
1 tablespoon butter
2 tablespoons consommé
2 whole eggs
2 egg yolks
   Half-and-half (optional)

Mix all ingredients in a blender. Add cream if needed to make a liquid puree. Pour mixture into a mold or pan which has been oiled and lined with waxed paper. Cover with foil and set in a pan of cold water. Bake at 300° for 1½ hours. Do not let water in pan boil. Turn gateau out onto a plate and slice about ½ inch thick.

Serve on thin buttered toast rounds with chopped lobster or crabmeat covered with a rich white sauce. Yield: about 2 cups.

CHOPPED CHICKEN LIVERS

3 tablespoons butter or margarine, divided
1 whole clove garlic
2 onions, finely minced
1 pound chicken livers
   Salt and pepper
2 hard-cooked eggs
¼ cup melted butter or margarine
1 tablespoon sherry (optional)

Heat 2 tablespoons butter and garlic, with a wooden pick in it, in skillet. Add onions and sauté until tender and yellow; do not brown. Discard garlic; turn onions into a bowl. Add a bit more butter to skillet and sauté livers until done: do not overcook. Stir in seasonings; put mixture and eggs through the finest blade of meat grinder. Blend in melted butter and sherry, stirring until smooth. May be made a day ahead. Leftovers freeze well. Yield: 12 servings.

VELVET CHICKEN LIVER PÂTÉ

½ pound chicken livers
2 tablespoons melted butter or margarine
⅓ to ½ cup chicken broth
2 hard-cooked eggs, chopped
   Salt, pepper, and seasoned salt to taste
2 (3-ounce) packages cream cheese, softened
2 tablespoons dry sherry
   Stuffed olives, sliced
   Parsley

Sauté livers in butter about 10 minutes or until just tender. Stir in broth, and swirl in pan a minute; then put in container of electric blender. Add eggs, and blend until smooth.

Blend seasonings into cream cheese; then combine with liver mixture. Add sherry and blend well. Put pâté in an oiled mold or bowl. Chill. Unmold and garnish with olives and parsley. Yield: about 2½ cups.

BACON-WRAPPED CHICKEN LIVERS

12 chicken livers
  Butter
  Salt and pepper
12 water chestnuts, sliced
 6 bacon slices

Sauté chicken livers in butter; salt and pepper generously. Cool enough to handle. Place a slice of water chestnut on each side of each chicken liver. Wrap in one-half slice of bacon; fasten with wooden pick. Place on a shallow baking sheet. Bake at 350° until bacon is brown. (Do not overcook, as livers are already cooked.) Drain fat from livers; put in chafing dish for serving, using burner to keep hot. Yield: 1 dozen.

CURRIED CHICKEN-CHEESE PIE

2 envelopes (2 tablespoons)
    unflavored gelatin
1 cup milk
2 chicken bouillon cubes
2 eggs, separated
½ teaspoon Ac'cent
2 teaspoons curry powder
3 cups creamed cottage cheese
2 tablespoons lemon juice
2 cups finely chopped cooked
    chicken
¼ cup chutney
¼ cup diced pimiento
2 tablespoons minced onion
1 cup whipping cream, whipped
    Radishes and scallions

Sprinkle gelatin over milk in saucepan; add bouillon cubes and egg yolks, mixing well. Place over low heat, and stir constantly until gelatin and bouillon cubes dissolve and mixture thickens slightly (about 5 minutes). Remove from heat; stir in Ac'cent and curry powder.
   Sieve or beat cottage cheese at high speed of electric mixer until smooth; stir into gelatin mixture. Stir in lemon juice, chicken, chutney, pimiento, and onion. Chill, if necessary, until mixture mounds

slightly when dropped from a spoon.
   Beat egg whites until stiff but not dry; fold into gelatin mixture. Fold in whipped cream. Spoon into an 8-inch springform pan. Chill until firm. Remove sides of pan, and garnish pie with radishes and scallions before serving. Yield: 24 servings.

CHICKEN ALMOND SWIRLS

1 (8-ounce) can refrigerated crescent
    dinner rolls
1 (4¾-ounce) can chicken spread
1 tablespoon diced toasted almonds
1 tablespoon mayonnaise
½ teaspoon lemon juice
  Seasoned salt

Separate dough into 4 rectangles; press along perforations to seal. Combine remaining ingredients; spread on rectangles. Roll up each rectangle, jelly roll fashion, starting with long side. Slice each roll into 8 slices. Place, cut side down, on greased cookie sheet. Bake at 375° for 12 to 15 minutes or until golden brown. Serve warm. Yield: about 2½ dozen.

POLYNESIAN CHICKEN WINGS

1 pound chicken wings
1 (8-ounce) jar commercial sweet-sour
    salad dressing

Cut chicken wings so that you have a drumstick and wingtip. Discard the wingtip, or cook for broth, or reserve for some other use.
   Dip chicken portions in sweet-sour salad dressing. Arrange pieces so that they do not touch on an aluminum foil lined cookie sheet. Bake at 325° for 1 hour, basting occasionally with the sauce, so that wings bake golden brown. Do not elevate the heat, or the chicken will brown too quickly. Keep chicken warm in a chafing dish. Yield: 12 servings.

Casseroles and Pies

CHICKEN MACIEL

2 pounds chicken breasts
1 tablespoon curry powder
½ teaspoon paprika
3 tablespoons butter or margarine
1 pint half-and-half
1 teaspoon cornstarch
2 tablespoons cooking sherry
   Salt and pepper to taste
1 cup cooked rice
½ to 1 cup shredded Swiss cheese

Cover chicken breasts with boiling salted water and simmer until tender. Remove from broth and chill.

Remove meat from cold chicken and cut into large pieces. Sauté chicken, curry, and paprika in butter until chicken is well coated with curry and paprika. Remove chicken from pan; add half-and-half and bring to a boil. Dissolve cornstarch in sherry and gradually add to hot cream. Add salt and pepper to taste. Stir in chicken and cooked rice. Place in a 1½-quart casserole. Sprinkle top generously with Swiss cheese, and bake at 375° about 10 minutes or until cheese is bubbly. Yield: 4 to 6 servings.

CHICKEN-SPINACH NOODLE CASSEROLE

1 (5-pound) hen
¾ (8-ounce) package spinach egg noodles
1 cup chopped onion
1 cup chopped green pepper
½ cup melted margarine
1 (8-ounce) package pasteurized process American cheese
½ cup sliced stuffed olives
1 (4-ounce) can sliced mushrooms, drained

Cook hen until tender; reserve stock. Boil noodles in chicken stock until tender; set noodles aside to absorb as much stock as possible. Remove chicken from bones; dice enough to make 4 cups.

Sauté onion and green pepper in margarine. Melt cheese in top of double boiler; add to onion and green pepper. Drain noodles, reserving 1 cup stock to add to casserole. Combine all ingredients; pour into a greased 2½-quart casserole. Bake at 350° about 30 minutes. Yield: 12 servings.

CRUNCHY CHICKEN CASSEROLE

2½ to 3 cups chopped cooked chicken
1 (4-ounce) can mushroom stems and pieces, drained
2 (14½-ounce) cans cut asparagus, drained
1 (8½-ounce) can water chestnuts, drained and thinly sliced
⅛ teaspoon pepper
1 (10¾-ounce) can condensed cream of chicken soup
1 (10¾-ounce) can condensed cream of mushroom soup
½ cup mayonnaise
¼ cup chopped ripe olives
1½ cups buttered cracker crumbs

Combine all ingredients except cracker crumbs; mix gently. Spoon into a 2-quart casserole; top with cracker crumbs. Bake at 350° for 45 minutes. Yield: 8 servings.

SCALLOPED CHICKEN AND RICE

1 (4- or 5-pound) chicken, cooked
    and boned
2 cups cooked rice
3 cups chicken broth
2 cups dry bread crumbs
3 large eggs, well beaten
½ cup finely diced green pepper
½ cup chopped pimiento
1 (10¾-ounce) can condensed cream
    of mushroom soup

Combine all ingredients except soup.
Place mixture in a large, buttered,
baking dish. Spread soup over top. Cover
and bake at 325° for 45 minutes. Yield: 6
servings.

CHICKEN AND RICE MEXICALI

2 tablespoons all-purpose flour
1 teaspoon garlic salt
1 teaspoon paprika
8 large pieces frying chicken
    Salad oil
1 cup finely chopped onion
1 clove garlic, minced
½ cup finely chopped
    green pepper
1 teaspoon chili powder
2 cups regular rice, uncooked
1 (1-pound 14-ounce) can tomatoes
1 (4-ounce) can green chiles,
    chopped
1 (10-ounce) package frozen whole
    kernel corn
3½ cups chicken broth
1 teaspoon salt
½ teaspoon pepper

Combine flour, garlic salt, and paprika;
dredge chicken in flour mixture and
brown slowly in hot salad oil. Remove
chicken. Measure oil left in pan and
return ¼ cup to pan. Add onion, garlic,
green pepper, and chili powder. Cook
until vegetables are soft.

Add rice to vegetables; cook a few
minutes until heated, stirring
occasionally. Stir in all remaining
ingredients except chicken. Spoon into
shallow casserole. Tuck chicken pieces
into rice mixture. Cover. Bake at 375°
about 50 to 60 minutes until rice is
tender and liquid is absorbed. Yield: 8
servings.

CHICKEN DIVAN

2 whole chicken breasts
    Pinch rosemary
    Salt and pepper to taste
1 cup water
2 tablespoons melted butter or
    margarine
2 tablespoons all-purpose
    flour
1 cup milk
1 egg yolk, beaten
    Juice of ½ lemon
½ teaspoon grated
    lemon rind
½ cup mayonnaise
2 (10-ounce) packages frozen
    spinach, asparagus, or broccoli,
    cooked and drained
    Grated Parmesan cheese

Place chicken breasts, rosemary, salt,
pepper, and water in a saucepan; bring to
a boil. Cover and cook over low heat for
10 to 15 minutes or until chicken is
tender. Drain, reserving chicken broth.
Bone and chop chicken, set aside.
  Combine butter and flour; cook over
low heat, stirring constantly, until
smooth. Combine milk and ½ cup
reserved chicken broth; gradually add to
flour mixture. Cook, stirring constantly,
until smooth and thickened. Blend in egg
yolk, lemon juice, and lemon rind; cook 1
minute, stirring constantly. Add
mayonnaise, mixing well.
  Layer half of spinach, chicken, and
sauce in a lightly greased 2-quart
casserole. Repeat layers; sprinkle with
cheese. Bake at 350° for 30 minutes.
Yield: 6 to 8 servings.

CHICKEN LIVERS AND RICE

4 tablespoons butter or margarine, divided
3 tablespoons minced onion
1⅓ cups precooked rice
½ pound frozen or fresh chicken livers, cut into 1-inch pieces
Seasoned all-purpose flour
1 (10¾-ounce) can condensed cream of chicken soup
½ cup milk
1 tablespoon chopped parsley

Melt 1 tablespoon butter in saucepan; add onion and cook until tender. Add to rice; cook as package directs. Dredge chicken livers lightly in flour; sauté in remaining 3 tablespoons butter in skillet until browned on each side. Combine livers, rice, soup, milk, and parsley in a 1½-quart casserole. Bake for 30 minutes at 375° until hot and bubbly. Yield: 2 to 4 servings.

LAHANA TABUK

3 whole chicken breasts, boned and chopped
½ cup olive oil
½ cup chopped green onions and tops
2 large garlic cloves, chopped
2 tablespoons uncooked cream of wheat
1 cup mashed tomatoes, either canned or fresh
½ cup white wine
1 cup cooked and mashed garbanzo beans
1 teaspoon black pepper
½ teaspoon white pepper
Salt to taste
½ cup chopped fresh parsley
15 to 18 cabbage leaves

Sauté chopped chicken in olive oil until tender. Put chicken aside, leaving oil in skillet and adding more oil if needed. Sauté chopped onion, garlic, and cream of wheat. When mixture is a light yellow brown, add tomatoes immediately. Stir and cook until tomatoes are done. Add wine, garbanzos, and sautéed chicken; mix well. Add peppers, salt, and parsley; form into a doughlike mass and set aside.

Wash and dry cabbage leaves; cut away the hard end. At opposite side of leaf, place a small amount of chicken mixture. Roll and secure with a wooden pick.

Place cabbage rolls in a shallow dish; bake at 200° for 8 to 10 minutes or until cabbage leaves begin to wilt. Serve warm or cold. Yield: 6 to 8 servings.

CHICKEN AND RICE CASSEROLE

2 (10¾-ounce) cans condensed cream of mushroom soup
1 cup half-and-half
1 cup shredded sharp Cheddar cheese
½ cup grated Parmesan cheese
1½ tablespoons minced onion
1 tablespoon prepared mustard
¼ teaspoon rosemary
⅛ teaspoon pepper
4 cups cooked rice
4 cups cubed cooked chicken
1 (20-ounce) can carrots and peas
1 (3-ounce) can French-fried onion rings

Combine soup and half-and-half; cook over low heat until hot, being careful not to boil. Stir in cheeses, onion, and seasonings; remove from heat. Combine sauce, rice, and chicken. Alternate layers of rice mixture with carrots and peas in lightly buttered 3-quart casserole. Sprinkle top with onion rings. Bake, uncovered, at 350° for 15 to 20 minutes or until mixture is bubbly. Yield: 10 servings.

TARRAGON CHICKEN CASSEROLE

1 (2½- to 3-pound) chicken, cut into
    pieces
1 to 2 medium onions, chopped
1½ teaspoons tarragon
¼ teaspoon poultry seasoning
1¼ teaspoons salt
¼ teaspoon pepper
1 (10¾-ounce) can condensed cream
    of chicken soup
¼ cup milk
¼ cup slivered almonds (optional)

Place chicken in a lightly greased
13- × 9-inch baking pan; do not overlap.
Sprinkle onion, tarragon, poultry
seasoning, salt, and pepper over chicken.

Combine soup and milk, stirring well;
spoon over chicken. Bake, uncovered, at
375° for 40 minutes or until chicken is
tender. Sprinkle with almonds, if desired,
and bake an additional 10 minutes.
Yield: 6 servings.

VATAPA

1 hen or 2 fryers
    Water
2 green peppers, chopped
2 large onions, chopped
1 cup melted margarine
2 (8-ounce) packages spaghetti
1 (16-ounce) can tiny peas,
    drained
1 (16-ounce) can tomatoes
1 (2-ounce) jar pimientos,
    chopped
1 pound pasteurized process
    American cheese
    Salt and pepper to taste

Cover the hen or fryers with water in a
large saucepan. Simmer approximately 3
hours on very low heat. Add water as
chicken cooks so that you have 3 cups
broth when chicken is done. Let cool in
broth. Sauté green pepper and onion in
margarine for 4 or 5 minutes. Remove
chicken from bones. Cook spaghetti in

chicken broth; add water if needed. Do
not drain. Add peas, tomatoes, pimientos,
cheese, chicken, green pepper, onion, salt,
and pepper. Put in casserole. Bake at
325° for 30 minutes.

Note: This dish can be made in advance
and frozen for later use. To freeze, omit
the last 30 minutes in the oven. To serve,
thaw and cook at 325° for 30 minutes.
Yield: 12 to 15 servings.

CHICKEN-ASPARAGUS CASSEROLE

2 (14½-ounce) cans asparagus spears,
    drained
6 whole chicken breasts, cooked and
    cut into bite-size pieces
1 medium onion, chopped
1 (4-ounce) can sliced mushrooms,
    drained
½ cup melted margarine
2 (10¾-ounce) cans
    condensed cream
    of mushroom soup
¾ cup evaporated milk
1 (8-ounce) package Cheddar cheese,
    shredded
¼ teaspoon hot sauce
2 tablespoons soy sauce
½ teaspoon pepper
1 teaspoon Ac'cent
2 tablespoons chopped
    pimiento
½ cup chopped almonds
    Hot cooked rice

Place asparagus in a greased 13- ×
9-inch pan; cover with chicken. Sauté
onion and mushrooms in margarine. Add
remaining ingredients except almonds
and rice; simmer until cheese melts.

Pour sauce over chicken; sprinkle with
almonds. Bake at 350° for 35 to 45
minutes or until bubbly. Serve over rice.
Yield: 8 to 10 servings.

HOT CHICKEN SALAD CASEROLE

4 cups diced cooked chicken
2 (10¾-ounce) cans condensed cream
    of chicken soup
2 cups diced celery
¼ cup minced onion
¾ cup slivered almonds
1 cup mayonnaise
¾ cup chicken stock
1 teaspoon salt
½ teaspoon pepper
¼ cup lemon juice
6 hard-cooked eggs, finely chopped
1 cup buttered cracker crumbs

Combine all ingredients except cracker
crumbs; place in a 3½-quart casserole.
Cover with cracker crumbs. Bake at 350°
for 40 minutes. Yield: 10 to 12 servings.

CHICKEN AND HAM BAKE

¼ cup chopped onion
¼ cup melted margarine
2 tablespoons parsley flakes
½ teaspoon poultry seasoning
¼ teaspoon pepper
1 cup cracker crumbs
¼ cup water
1 egg
1½ cups diced cooked chicken
¼ pound shredded pasteurized
    process American cheese
6 slices boiled ham
¼ pound sliced pasteurized process
    American cheese

Sauté onion in margarine until tender.
Add parsley, seasonings, cracker crumbs,
water, egg, chicken, and shredded cheese;
mix well. Place a large spoonful of
stuffing in center of each ham slice. Fold
ham over stuffing. Secure with wooden
picks. Place in a 6- × 10- × 2-inch
baking dish and cover with foil. Bake at
350° for 20 to 30 minutes. Remove foil
and lay slices of cheese on centers of ham
rolls. Bake about 5 minutes more until
cheese melts. Yield: 6 servings.

CHICKEN SOUFFLÉ

8 slices day-old bread
2 cups diced cooked chicken
½ cup mayonnaise
1 cup diced celery
¾ cup finely chopped onion
¾ cup finely chopped green pepper
    Salt and pepper to taste
4 eggs, beaten
3 cups milk
1 (10¾-ounce) can condensed cream
    of mushroom soup
1 cup shredded cheese

Cut 4 slices of bread into cubes; remove
crusts from the other 4 slices. Line
bottom of a 10½- × 7- × 1½-inch baking
dish with bread cubes.
    Combine chicken, mayonnaise, celery,
onion, and green pepper; season to taste.
Spread this mixture over bread cubes.
Cover with bread slices. Combine eggs
and milk and pour over bread slices;
cover and place in refrigerator overnight.
    One hour before serving time, bake at
350° for 15 minutes. Pour undiluted soup
over mixture and bake for 30 minutes.
Sprinkle top with cheese and bake an
additional 15 minutes. Yield: 10 to 12
servings.

ALPINE CHICKEN CASSEROLE

4 cups chopped, cooked chicken
2 cups sliced celery
2 cups toasted bread cubes
1 cup salad dressing or mayonnaise
½ cup milk
¼ cup chopped onion
1 teaspoon salt
    Dash pepper
1 (8-ounce) package sliced Swiss
    cheese, cut into thin strips
¼ cup sliced almonds

Combine all ingredients except almonds.
Spoon into a lightly greased 2-quart
casserole; sprinkle with almonds. Bake at
350° for 40 minutes. Yield: 6 to 8
servings.

19

HOT CHICKEN CASSEROLE

2 cups chopped cooked chicken
2 cups finely chopped celery
½ cup chopped pecans or almonds
½ cup chopped green pepper
   (optional)
½ tablespoon chopped pimiento
   (optional)
2 tablespoons minced onion
½ to 1 tablespoon salt
2 to 6 tablespoons lemon juice
¾ cup mayonnaise
½ cup shredded Cheddar cheese
1 to 3 cups crushed potato chips

Combine all ingredients except cheese
and potato chips in a 3-quart casserole
dish. Top with cheese and potato chips.
Bake at 350° for 15 to 25 minutes or
until cheese is melted and celery is
tender. Yield: 4 to 6 servings.

CHICKEN NOODLE TETRAZZINI

1 (4-pound) chicken or 8 whole
   chicken breasts
1 teaspoon salt
2 quarts water
1 (10-ounce) package noodles
1 medium green pepper, chopped
1 medium onion, minced
1 (4-ounce) can sliced mushrooms
½ pound melted butter or margarine
⅔ cup all-purpose flour
2 cups milk
½ pound shredded pasteurized
   process American cheese
½ pound shredded sharp Cheddar
   cheese
   Salt and pepper to taste

Cook chicken in salted water until
tender. Remove from broth; cool, bone,
and cut into small pieces. Strain broth,
let cool, and remove fat; reserve chicken
broth.
   Cook noodles in 1 quart chicken broth.
Sauté green pepper, onion, and
mushrooms in butter until tender; add
flour and blend well. Add milk and 2
cups broth; cook until sauce is thick. Stir

in cheeses and cook over low heat until
cheeses melt.
   Combine chicken, noodles, and cheese
sauce; add salt and pepper. Place in a
2½- or 3-quart casserole; bake at 350° for
40 minutes. Yield: 12 servings.

PIMIENTO-CHICKEN LOAF

1 egg, well beaten
½ teaspoon salt
¼ cup evaporated milk, scalded
1½ cups cooked mashed potatoes
1½ cups cooked, diced chicken
2 whole pimientos, chopped
¼ teaspoon paprika

Combine egg, salt, evaporated milk, and
mashed potatoes. Add chicken, chopped
pimientos, and paprika.
   Put mixture into a greased baking
dish; bake at 350° until casserole is
browned. Yield: 6 servings.

CHICKEN-MACARONI CASSEROLE

2 cups elbow macaroni
2 medium onions, chopped
1 green pepper, chopped
¼ cup salad oil
1 small clove garlic, minced
1 quart chicken broth
2½ cups diced cooked chicken
1 (20-ounce) can cream-style corn
2 (8-ounce) cans tomato sauce
2½ teaspoons chili powder
2 (4-ounce) cans mushrooms,
   drained
1½ teaspoons salt
½ cup grated Parmesan cheese
¼ cup butter or margarine

Cook macaroni as directed on package;
drain. Sauté onion and green pepper in
oil; do not brown. Add garlic, and
combine with macaroni, chicken broth,
chicken, corn, tomato sauce, chili powder,
mushrooms, and salt. Bring to simmering
point. Place in buttered 2-quart casserole.
Top with cheese and dot with butter.
Bake at 350° about 25 minutes or until
delicately brown. Yield: 4 to 6 servings.

CURRIED CHICKEN CASSEROLE

2 (10¾-ounce) cans condensed cream
  of chicken soup
1 cup mayonnaise
½ teaspoon curry powder
1 teaspoon lemon juice
  Salt and pepper to taste
2 (10-ounce) packages frozen
  chopped broccoli, cooked and
  drained
4 cups chopped cooked chicken
  Buttered bread crumbs

Combine chicken soup, mayonnaise,
curry powder, lemon juice, salt, and
pepper; mix well.

Layer half of broccoli, chicken, and
soup mixture in a lightly greased,
2-quart, shallow casserole; repeat layers.
Sprinkle with bread crumbs. Bake at
350° for 30 minutes. Yield: 6 servings.

OLD-STYLE CHICKEN TETRAZZINI

1 (4-pound) chicken, cut up
1 medium onion
1 teaspoon peppercorns
  Salt
1 teaspoon sugar
1 bay leaf
1 stalk celery with tops
5 quarts water
1 (16-ounce) package spaghetti
2 cups sliced mushrooms
1 large onion, chopped
1 green pepper, chopped
1 (2-ounce) jar pimiento, chopped
2 tablespoons melted margarine
  White Sauce
  Grated Parmesan cheese

Combine chicken, whole onion,
peppercorns, 1 tablespoon salt, sugar, bay
leaf, celery, and water; simmer about 3
hours or until chicken is tender. Remove
chicken from bones and cut into small
pieces; set aside.

Strain broth, reserving 2 cups for
White Sauce; bring remaining broth to a
boil, and add salt to taste. Cook spaghetti
in boiling broth until tender.

Sauté mushrooms and chopped
vegetables in margarine; set aside.
Combine chicken, spaghetti, vegetables,
and White Sauce. Spoon mixture into a
3-quart casserole; top with Parmesan
cheese. Bake at 400° for 20 minutes.
Yield: 10 to 12 servings.

White Sauce:

¼ cup melted margarine
¼ cup all-purpose flour
2 cups chicken broth
1 cup half-and-half
  Salt and pepper to taste

Combine margarine and flour; cook over
low heat until bubbly. Slowly add
chicken broth and half-and-half, stirring
constantly. Cook until smooth and thick;
season to taste with salt and pepper.
Yield: about 3 cups.

CHICKEN PIE DELUXE

2 cups commercial herb-seasoned
  stuffing, divided
½ cup melted butter or margarine
½ cup milk
1 (10¾-ounce) can condensed cream
  of celery soup
1½ cups diced cooked chicken
¾ cup cooked peas
1 tablespoon minced onion
  Dash pepper
  Chopped parsley

Combine 1¼ cups stuffing and butter;
press mixture to bottom and sides of
9-inch pie plate. Combine milk and soup
in saucepan; add chicken, peas, onion,
and pepper. Heat and turn into pie shell.

Bake at 425° about 10 minutes or until
bubbly. Crumble remaining ¾ cup
stuffing; arrange crumbs around border.
Sprinkle center with parsley. Yield: 6
servings.

FLAKY CRUST CHICKEN PIE

1 teaspoon salt
1 (2½- to 3-pound) broiler-fryer
    chicken, cut up
2 tablespoons melted butter or
    margarine
2 cups water
1 cup milk
3 tablespoons all-purpose flour
    Pastry
3 hard-cooked eggs,
    sliced

Salt chicken pieces; broil in butter, turn chicken, and add 2 cups water. Cover and simmer until chicken is tender. Remove chicken from broth, and bone it. Add milk to chicken broth; thicken with flour.

Roll one-fourth of Pastry ⅛ inch thick; cut to fit sides of 3-quart baking pan, having pastry higher than pan to form edge. Layer chicken and eggs in pan; add sauce.

Roll out remaining pastry; place on top of pie, folding under around edge; flute with fingers. Cut a cross in center of pastry, and fold triangles back to allow steam to escape.

Bake at 450° for 10 minutes; then reduce heat to 350° and bake 15 additional minutes or until pastry is a delicate brown. Yield: 4 to 6 servings.

Pastry:

1 cup plus 2 tablespoons
    all-purpose flour
½ teaspoon salt
6 tablespoons shortening
2½ tablespoons ice water

Combine flour and salt in bowl. Cut in 4 tablespoons shortening very thoroughly; then add remaining shortening and cut until mixture has coarse crumbs the size of large peas. Sprinkle with water, a small amount at a time, tossing mixture with a fork to moisten completely. When all particles are moistened, press into a ball.

CHICKEN PARTY PIE

1½ cups cooked, chopped chicken
1 (8¼-ounce) can pineapple tidbits,
    drained
1 cup chopped pecans or walnuts
½ cup chopped celery
1 cup commercial sour cream
⅔ cup mayonnaise
    Pastry
3 tablespoons shredded sharp
    pasteurized process American
    cheese
    Stuffed olives, sliced

Combine chicken, pineapple, pecans, and celery. Combine sour cream and mayonnaise; add ⅔ cup to chicken mixture and blend. Prepare Pastry; pour mixture into baked pie shell, top with remaining sour cream mixture, and garnish with cheese and olives. Yield: 6 servings.

Pastry:

1½ cups all-purpose flour
⅛ teaspoon salt
½ cup shortening
¼ cup water or milk
⅓ cup shredded sharp pasteurized
    process American cheese

Combine dry ingredients; cut in shortening. Add liquid, blend in cheese, and mix lightly. Roll out on floured surface. Place pastry in a 9-inch piepan and prick with a fork. Bake at 425° for 12 to 15 minutes or until delicately browned.

CHICKEN PIE

Pastry for double-crust pie
6 tablespoons butter
6 tablespoons all-purpose flour
½ teaspoon salt
¼ teaspoon pepper
1¾ cups chicken broth
⅔ cup milk or half-and-half
2 cups diced cooked chicken

Prepare pastry; divide into two parts, two-thirds in one part and one-third in other. Roll out and place two-thirds in a 10- × 6- × 1½-inch baking pan.

Melt butter; add flour and seasonings. Cook over low heat until frothy. Add liquids and cook slowly until thickened. Add chicken. Pour into pastry lined pan. Top with rest of pastry. Pinch edges together. Bake at 425° for 35 minutes. Yield: 6 servings.

LITTLE BISCUIT-TOPPED CHICKEN PIES

1 (5-ounce) can boned chicken
6 small white onions, peeled
1 cup biscuit mix
2 tablespoons melted butter or margarine
2 tablespoons all-purpose flour
¼ teaspoon salt
   Dash pepper
¼ teaspoon Worcestershire sauce
1 chicken bouillon cube
½ cup milk
2 teaspoons sherry
½ cup minced celery
   Milk
   Parsley (optional)

Cut chicken into bite-size pieces; set aside. Cook onions, covered, in boiling salted water for 10 minutes or until tender; drain.

Prepare biscuit mix according to package directions; roll out dough and cut into 2-inch circles.

Combine butter and flour in top of double boiler; cook until bubbly. Add salt, pepper, Worcestershire sauce, bouillon cube, and ½ cup milk; cook, stirring constantly, until smooth and thick. Remove from heat, and blend in sherry.

Arrange chicken, onions, and celery in 2 individual casseroles or a 1-quart casserole; add sauce, and top with biscuits. Brush biscuits with milk. Bake at 425° for 30 minutes or until biscuits are browned. Garnish with parsley, if desired. Yield: 2 servings.

CHICKEN PIE SUPERB

1 (4- to 5-pound) chicken
1 carrot, diced
1 onion, diced
1 stalk celery, chopped
1 sprig parsley, chopped
1 teaspoon rosemary
½ teaspoon salt
⅛ teaspoon pepper
5 tablespoons all-purpose flour
1 cup half-and-half
1 teaspoon salt
¼ teaspoon pepper
1 (16-ounce) can green peas, drained
½ cup butter or margarine
1 (4-ounce) can mushroom slices, drained
   Pastry for a 1-crust pie

Place chicken on rack in container half-filled with hot water. Add carrot, onion, celery, parsley, rosemary, ½ teaspoon salt, and pepper. Partly cover with a lid, and simmer 3 to 4 hours or until tender, turning occasionally. Cool chicken in broth, breast side down. Skim off excess fat from stock. Remove chicken from broth, and strain broth, reserving 1½ cups. Bone chicken, and set aside.

Make a sauce by blending flour with ¼ cup of the broth in a saucepan. Stir in slowly the remaining broth and half-and-half. Cook until thick, stirring constantly to avoid lumps. Season with salt and pepper. Place chicken and peas in a baking dish. Add sauce; dot butter over sauce and chicken. Add mushrooms. Cover sauce and chicken with pastry rolled ⅛ inch thick.

Press pastry against sides of dish and cut gashes across the top. Bake at 425° for 12 to 15 minutes. Yield: 6 servings.

Entrées

GINGERED CHICKEN IN WINE

4 whole chicken breasts, split
¼ cup soy sauce
¾ cup red wine
¼ teaspoon ground dried oregano
1 clove garlic, sliced
¼ cup salad oil
¼ cup water
1 teaspoon ground ginger
1 tablespoon firmly packed brown
    sugar
    Parsley flakes

Place chicken breasts, flat side down, in a shallow casserole. Combine remaining ingredients; pour over chicken. Bake, covered, at 350° for 1 hour. Yield: 4 servings.

CHICKEN PROVENÇALE

2 tablespoons salad oil
1 broiler-fryer chicken, cut in
    serving-size pieces
½ cup chopped onion
½ clove garlic, minced or crushed
1 green pepper, chopped
1 eggplant, pared and sliced
2 tomatoes, peeled and sliced
2 teaspoons dried leaf basil
¼ cup chopped parsley

Heat oil in a large skillet; add chicken and brown on all sides. Remove chicken from skillet, and place in a shallow baking dish.

Add onion, garlic, and green pepper to skillet; cook until tender, and spoon over chicken.

Arrange eggplant and tomato slices on top of chicken. Sprinkle with basil and parsley. Cover and bake at 375° for 1 hour or until tender. Yield: 4 servings.

BAKED CHICKEN AND RICE

1 whole chicken breast, split
    Melted butter or margarine
½ cup uncooked regular rice
1 (10½-ounce) can condensed chicken
    broth
⅛ teaspoon celery seeds
⅛ teaspoon celery salt
½ teaspoon parsley flakes
½ teaspoon green pepper flakes
1 (6-ounce) can water chestnuts,
    sliced
    Salt and pepper to taste

Brush chicken with butter; place in a shallow casserole and bake at 350° about 30 minutes. Add remaining ingredients; cover and bake at 350° about 30 minutes or until chicken is tender and rice is done. Yield: 2 servings.

CHICKEN WITH ROSEMARY

2½ to 3 pounds chicken breasts and
    thighs, skinned
    All-purpose flour
    Salt and pepper to taste
    About 2 to 3 teaspoons dried
    rosemary
2 chicken bouillon cubes
1 cup water

Coat chicken with flour; place in a buttered baking pan. Season with salt, pepper, and rosemary. Crumble bouillon cubes between chicken pieces; add water, pouring into a corner of pan. Cook, covered with foil at 350° for 1 hour. Uncover; baste with drippings, and brown under broiler. Yield: 6 to 8 servings.

CHICKEN WITH CABBAGE AND WINE

¼ cup chicken broth
½ cup chopped onion
1 (3- to 4-pound) chicken, cut up
1 cup dry white wine
1½ teaspoons salt, divided
⅛ teaspoon pepper
6 cups shredded cabbage
1 tablespoon lemon juice
¼ cup drained, chopped pimiento

Heat chicken broth in a small saucepan over low heat; add onion and cook until tender, stirring occasionally.

Place chicken in a deep 3-quart casserole. Combine onion mixture, wine, 1 teaspoon salt, and pepper; pour over chicken. Bake, uncovered, at 350° for 45 minutes, basting occasionally.

Add cabbage, ½ teaspoon salt, and lemon juice to chicken; cover and continue baking 20 minutes, stirring once or twice. Stir in pimiento; cover and bake 5 minutes longer. Yield: about 6 servings.

BAKED CHICKEN IN WINE

2 (2½- to 3-pound) chickens, cut into pieces
All-purpose flour
1 cup salad oil
1 clove garlic, minced
1 (6-ounce) can sliced mushrooms, undrained
Salt and pepper to taste
Garlic salt to taste
1 (⅘-quart) bottle white wine
Cooked wild rice

Dredge chicken in flour. Put ½ inch salad oil in skillet; brown and remove garlic. Fry chicken until brown; remove from skillet and place in large baking dish. Add mushrooms to skillet and brown thoroughly. Pour garlic, mushrooms, and oil over chicken; add salt, pepper, and garlic salt. Pour wine over chicken and bake at 325° for 1 hour. Serve gravy over wild rice. Yield: 6 servings.

CHICKEN HAWAIIAN

3 pounds broiler-fryer chicken pieces
1 teaspoon salt
1 egg
⅓ cup frozen pineapple-orange juice concentrate, thawed
4 cups cornflakes, crushed, or 1 cup cornflake crumbs
½ cup flaked coconut
½ teaspoon curry powder
¼ cup melted margarine
Pineapple rings

Arrange chicken in a shallow baking pan; sprinkle with salt. Combine egg and fruit juice in a small bowl, and beat well; pour over chicken pieces. Let stand in refrigerator about 1 hour, turning chicken pieces once.

Combine crushed cornflakes, coconut, and curry. Drain chicken pieces slightly; coat with cornflake mixture.

Place chicken, skin side up, in a single layer in a shallow baking pan. Drizzle with margarine. Bake at 350° about 1 hour or until fork tender. Garnish with pineapple rings. Yield: 6 to 8 servings.

MEXICAN CHICKEN

1 pint whipping cream
2 (10¾-ounce) cans condensed cream of mushroom soup
¼ teaspoon curry powder
¼ teaspoon chili powder
¼ teaspoon garlic powder
¼ teaspoon paprika
¼ teaspoon salt
¼ teaspoon pepper
2 (2- to 2½-pound) chickens, cut into pieces
Hot cooked rice or noodles

Combine whipping cream, soup, and seasonings. Arrange chicken in a lightly greased 13- × 9-inch baking pan; pour soup mixture over chicken. Bake at 350° for 1 hour or until chicken is done. Serve over rice. Yield: 8 servings.

PEANUT BUTTER-HONEY COATED CHICKEN

¼ cup margarine
⅓ cup smooth peanut butter
2 tablespoons honey
⅔ cup evaporated milk
6 tablespoons cornmeal
6 tablespoons all-purpose flour
1 teaspoon Ac'cent
1 teaspoon salt
½ teaspoon paprika
6 drumsticks
6 thighs

Melt margarine in foil lined baking pan at 375°; remove from oven.

Blend peanut butter, honey, and milk until smooth; set aside. Combine cornmeal, flour, Ac'cent, salt, and paprika. Dip chicken pieces in peanut butter mixture; coat well in cornmeal mixture. Place chicken in margarine and bake at 375° for 15 to 20 minutes; turn chicken and bake 15 to 20 minutes longer. Yield: 6 servings.

ELEGANT BAKED CHICKEN

½ cup all-purpose flour
½ teaspoon crushed dried oregano
½ teaspoon ground dried marjoram
½ teaspoon garlic salt
1 (2½- to 3-pound) broiler-fryer chicken, cut up
3 tablespoons salad oil
Salt and pepper to taste
Paprika to taste
1 small onion, diced
10 to 15 mushrooms, thinly sliced
¼ cup dry white wine
1 (8-ounce) carton commercial sour cream
1 cup shredded Swiss cheese

Completely submerge a 3-quart fired clay cooker in water for 15 minutes; pat dry.

Combine flour, oregano, marjoram, and garlic salt. Dredge chicken with flour mixture. Brown in hot oil; drain, reserving drippings. Season chicken with salt, pepper, and paprika; place in cooker. Cover with onion and mushrooms.

Add wine and sour cream to reserved drippings; blend well. Pour over chicken, and sprinkle with cheese. Cover and place in a cold oven; bake at 475° for 45 minutes or until chicken is tender. Yield: 6 servings.

BAKED MEDITERRANEAN CHICKEN

1 (2½- to 3-pound) broiler-fryer chicken, cut up
½ cup fine, dry bread crumbs
½ cup grated Parmesan cheese
2 teaspoons parsley flakes
1 teaspoon salt
½ teaspoon crushed dried oregano
¼ teaspoon ground dried thyme
¼ teaspoon pepper
¼ cup melted butter

Remove skin from chicken; combine all remaining ingredients except butter. Dip chicken in butter and then coat it evenly with crumb mixture. Arrange chicken so pieces don't touch in a greased shallow baking dish. Dot with butter. Bake at 350° until chicken is tender, about 1 hour. Yield: 4 servings.

CHICKEN DELIGHT

1 frying-size chicken, cut into pieces
All-purpose flour
Salt and pepper
1 cup catsup
¾ cup cola drink

Coat chicken pieces with flour which has been seasoned with salt and pepper. Place in a 13- × 9- × 2-inch pan. Combine catsup and cola drink; pour over chicken. Cover and bake at 350° about 1 hour or until chicken is tender. Yield: 4 to 6 servings.

CHICKEN VERMOUTH

4 whole chicken breasts
  Salt and pepper
½ cup melted butter or margarine
½ cup honey
¼ cup lemon juice
¼ cup dry vermouth

Place chicken breasts in heavy shallow pan. Season with salt and pepper. Broil chicken just enough to brown lightly; remove from oven and cover with melted butter to which has been added the honey, lemon juice, and vermouth. Cover with aluminum foil and bake at 325° for 1 hour. Yield: 4 servings.

SESAME BAKED CHICKEN

2 eggs, slightly beaten
1 tablespoon water
1 tablespoon soy sauce
1 teaspoon salt
¼ teaspoon pepper
6 large whole chicken breasts,
  skinned and boned
¼ cup all-purpose flour
½ cup sesame seeds
½ cup melted butter or margarine
  Mushroom Sauce

Combine eggs, water, soy sauce, salt, and pepper; mix well. Coat chicken with flour; dip into egg mixture and then into sesame seeds.

Pour melted butter into a shallow baking pan; add chicken, turning to coat. Bake at 400° for 40 to 50 minutes or

until golden brown and tender. Serve with mushroom sauce. Yield: 6 servings.

Mushroom Sauce:

1½ cups sliced fresh mushrooms
¼ cup butter or margarine
1 cup water, divided
2 tablespoons cornstarch
1 teaspoon Worcestershire sauce
1 teaspoon salt
  Dash pepper

Sauté mushrooms in butter until tender. Add ¾ cup water. Make a paste of cornstarch and ¼ cup water; blend into hot mushrooms and liquid, stirring constantly, until smooth and thickened. Add Worcestershire sauce, salt, and pepper. Yield: about 2 cups.

POLYNESIAN CHICKEN

6 whole chicken breasts, split
6 chicken thighs
6 chicken legs
3 (17-ounce) cans fruits for salads
1 (6-ounce) bottle soy sauce
1 clove garlic, crushed
3 (8-ounce) jars sweet-and-sour sauce
  Hot cooked rice

Remove skin and wash chicken; dry well with absorbent towels. Arrange chicken in a large, shallow roasting pan. Drain fruit, reserving syrup; store fruit in refrigerator.

Combine reserved syrup, soy sauce, and garlic; pour over chicken. Bake, uncovered, at 350° for 1 hour or until chicken is a rich golden brown; baste often.

Pour liquid from chicken into a large saucepan; add sweet-and-sour sauce, and bring to a boil over medium heat. Simmer about 40 minutes or until sauce thickens or is reduced to about 3½ cups; add fruit. Pour over chicken.

Bake, uncovered, at 350° for 30 minutes, basting often. Serve over rice. Yield: 12 servings.

TART 'N TANGY CHICKEN

2 whole chicken breasts, split
  Salt and pepper to taste
½ cup melted butter or margarine
  Juice of 2 lemons
1 tablespoon prepared mustard
1 teaspoon seasoned salt
⅓ cup chopped pepperoni or salami

Sprinkle chicken breasts with salt and pepper; place meaty side down in a shallow baking pan.

Combine butter, lemon juice, mustard, and seasoned salt; pour over chicken. Sprinkle with pepperoni or salami. Cover pan with heavy-duty aluminum foil and bake at 400° for 45 minutes.

Remove foil; turn chicken over. Broil for a few minutes to brown. Drippings may be served over green vegetables. Yield: 4 servings.

STUFFED CHICKEN BREASTS SAVANNAH

4 whole chicken breasts, skinned,
    boned, and halved
4 thin slices boiled ham, cut in half
4 thin slices Swiss cheese, cut in half
½ cup all-purpose flour, divided
1 egg, slightly beaten
⅔ cup fine dry bread crumbs
½ cup plus 2 tablespoons melted
    butter or margarine, divided
1 cup dry white wine
¼ cup finely chopped onion
½ teaspoon salt
  Pepper to taste
1 cup milk
1 cup half-and-half
  Chopped fresh parsley
  Hot cooked rice or noodles

Flatten chicken breasts with meat mallet. Place a slice of ham and cheese on each chicken breast; roll up and secure with wooden picks. Dredge each roll in ¼ cup flour, and dip in egg; coat well with bread crumbs.

Lightly brown on all sides in ¼ cup butter. Add wine; simmer, covered, for 20 minutes. Place rolls in a shallow baking dish, reserving drippings.

Sauté onion in 6 tablespoons butter until tender, stirring occasionally; blend in remaining ¼ cup flour, salt, and pepper. Gradually add milk and half-and-half, stirring constantly until smooth. Add reserved drippings; simmer, stirring constantly, until smooth and thickened.

Pour sauce over rolls; bake, uncovered, at 325° for 20 minutes. Garnish with parsley. Serve over rice. Yield: 8 servings.

CHICKEN CASSOULET

1 (3- to 4-pound) broiler-fryer
    chicken, cut into serving-size
    pieces
¼ cup seasoned all-purpose flour
6 tablespoons salad oil
1 small onion, sliced
1 clove garlic, minced
4 stalks celery, cut into 1-inch slices
4 carrots, cut into 1-inch slices
1 green pepper, cut into 1-inch slices
¼ pound fresh mushrooms
½ cup white wine
1 cup hot chicken broth or
    consomme
1 teaspoon salt
  Pepper

Place chicken in paper bag with flour; close bag and shake vigorously. Brown chicken well in salad oil; place in a 13- × 9- × 2-inch baking dish. Lightly sauté the onion, garlic, celery, carrot, green pepper, and mushrooms in oil left in skillet; place over chicken. Add wine and hot chicken broth. Sprinkle with salt and pepper. Cover tightly and bake at 325° for 1 hour or until tender. Yield: 4 servings.

CHICKEN-BROCCOLI BAKE

2 whole chicken breasts
2 tablespoons melted butter or
    margarine
1 (10-ounce) package frozen broccoli,
    cooked and drained
1 (10¾-ounce) can condensed cream
    of chicken soup
½ cup milk
½ cup shredded pasteurized process
    American cheese
¼ cup buttered bread crumbs
    Paprika

Arrange chicken in a 8- × 4- × 2-inch
baking dish. Drizzle butter over chicken.
Bake at 375° for 40 minutes. Place
cooked and drained broccoli around
chicken. Blend soup, milk, and cheese;
pour over chicken and broccoli. Top with
bread crumbs and sprinkle with paprika.
Bake 20 additional minutes. Yield: 2
servings.

CHICKEN BREASTS WELLINGTON

6 whole chicken breasts, boned and
    split
    Seasoned salt
    Seasoned pepper
1 (6-ounce) package long grain and
    wild rice
¼ cup grated orange peel
2 eggs, separated
3 (8-ounce) cans refrigerated
    crescent dinner rolls
1 tablespoon water
2 (10-ounce) jars red currant jelly
1 tablespoon prepared mustard
3 tablespoons port
¼ cup lemon juice

Pound chicken breasts with meat mallet;
sprinkle each with seasoned salt and
pepper.
    Cook rice according to package
directions for drier rice; add orange peel.
Cool. Beat egg whites until soft peaks
form; fold into rice mixture.
    On floured surface, roll 2 triangular

pieces of dinner roll dough into a circle.
Repeat with remaining rolls until you
have 12 circles. Place a chicken breast in
center of each circle. Spoon about ¼ cup
rice mixture over chicken; roll chicken
jelly roll fashion. Bring dough up over
stuffed breast. Moisten edges of dough
with water, and press together to seal.
    Place seam side down on large baking
sheet. Slightly beat egg yolks with water;
brush over dough. Bake, uncovered, at
375° for 45 to 50 minutes or until breasts
are tender. If dough browns too quickly,
cover loosely with foil.
    Heat currant jelly in saucepan;
gradually stir in mustard, wine, and
lemon juice. Serve warm with chicken.
Yield: 12 servings.

VEGETABLE-STUFFED CHICKEN BREASTS

2 tablespoons butter or margarine
¼ cup finely chopped celery
¼ cup finely chopped carrot
¼ cup finely chopped green pepper
1 medium onion, finely chopped
¼ teaspoon salt
1½ tablespoons chopped parsley
3 whole chicken breasts, boned
    Salt and pepper
3 tablespoons white wine
    Paprika

Melt butter in small skillet. Add celery,
carrot, green pepper, and onion. Sprinkle
with ¼ teaspoon salt. Cook over low heat
for 2 to 3 minutes; add parsley and mix
well.
    Place chicken breasts, skin side down,
on squares of aluminum foil. Sprinkle
very lightly with salt and pepper. Divide
vegetables among chicken breasts,
placing about 2½ tablespoons in center of
each. Fold sides of breast over mixture.
Pour 1 tablespoon white wine over each
breast and sprinkle with salt, pepper,
and paprika.
    Bring foil up over chicken; fold foil
securely to seal. Bake at 350° for 50 to 60
minutes. Yield: 3 servings.

BARBECUED BROILERS

¼ cup corn oil
¾ cup vinegar
2 tablespoons light corn oil syrup
2 tablespoons Worcestershire sauce
2 tablespoons paprika
1 tablespoon salt
2 cloves garlic, quartered
⅛ teaspoon cayenne pepper
Dash freshly ground black pepper
2 (2½- to 3½-pound) fryers, whole

Combine corn oil, vinegar, corn syrup, Worcestershire sauce, paprika, salt, garlic, cayenne, and pepper in saucepan. Bring to boil; reduce heat; simmer 5 minutes. Brush inside of each chicken with sauce. Tie legs and wings to body. Brush chickens with sauce. Place in dish; cover and let stand in refrigerator at least 1 hour.

Roast chickens breast side up on rack in shallow baking pan at 350° about 1½ hours, brushing occasionally with sauce. Yield: 6 to 8 servings.

ROAST CHICKEN EL GRECO

4 chicken wings
4 drumsticks
4 thighs
2 backs
¼ cup lemon juice
¼ cup olive oil
1½ teaspoons salt
¼ teaspoon pepper
¾ teaspoon crushed dried oregano

Arrange chicken parts in lightly greased large casserole in layers if necessary.

Thoroughly mix lemon juice, olive oil, salt, pepper, and oregano with fork in separate small bowl and drizzle this over all chicken pieces.

Cover casserole. Bake at 375° for 30 minutes. Uncover and finish baking as chicken browns (approximately 25 minutes longer). Yield: 6 to 8 servings.

CHICKEN TAHITIAN

6 whole chicken breasts
Salt and pepper to taste
2 tablespoons salad oil
1 (6-ounce) can frozen orange juice concentrate, thawed and undiluted
6 tablespoons melted butter or margarine
1¼ teaspoons ground ginger
1¼ teaspoons soy sauce
Hot cooked wild or regular rice
Pineapple slices

Season chicken lightly with salt and pepper. Put oil in a shallow baking pan; add chicken, and bake for 350° for 30 minutes.

Combine orange juice concentrate, butter, ginger, and soy sauce; simmer 3 minutes. Baste chicken with sauce; bake an additional 35 minutes, basting frequently with sauce.

Place chicken under broiler until golden brown. Serve with rice and remaining sauce. Garnish with pineapple slices. Yield: 6 servings.

SAVORY STUFFED CHICKEN BREASTS

⅓ cup chopped parsley
½ teaspoon salt
½ teaspoon ground dried thyme
⅛ teaspoon pepper
Dash celery salt
1½ cups ¼-inch cubed, day-old bread
5 tablespoons corn oil, divided
¼ cup chopped onion
4 whole chicken breasts, boned
¼ cup all-purpose flour
½ teaspoon paprika
Savory Sauce

Combine parsley, salt, thyme, pepper, and celery salt; toss with bread cubes. Heat 3 tablespoons oil in a small skillet; add onion and cook until tender, stirring frequently. Pour over seasoned bread cubes; mix well.

Place chicken, skin side down, on flat surface. Spoon stuffing into center of breasts; then lap sides together and fasten securely with wooden picks. Dust chicken lightly with flour and paprika.

Place 2 tablespoons oil in a baking dish or casserole. Heat at 350° about 10 minutes. Place chicken in hot oil; spoon Savory Sauce over chicken. Bake, uncovered, about 1 hour or until chicken is tender, basting occasionally. Yield: 4 servings.

Savory Sauce:

¼ **cup corn oil**
¼ **cup lemon juice**
¼ **teaspoon garlic salt**
¾ **teaspoon salt**
¼ **teaspoon ground dried thyme**
¼ **teaspoon ground dried marjoram**
⅛ **teaspoon pepper**

Combine all ingredients; mix well. Yield: about ½ cup.

HERBED CHICKEN

  Salt and pepper to taste
4 **whole chicken breasts**
1 **(10¾-ounce) can condensed cream of chicken soup**
¾ **cup white wine**
¼ **teaspoon ground dried thyme**
1 **tablespoon melted butter**
1 **(6-ounce) can water chestnuts, drained**
1 **(4-ounce) can mushrooms, drained**
2 **tablespoons chopped green pepper**

Salt and pepper chicken; place in shallow casserole. Combine soup, wine, thyme, and butter; pour over chicken. Cover; bake at 350° for 1 hour. Before serving, add water chestnuts, mushrooms, and green pepper. Yield: 4 servings.

ARROZ CON POLLO

1 **broiler-fryer chicken, cut into serving-size pieces**
1½ **teaspoons salt, divided**
½ **teaspoon paprika**
¼ **cup olive oil**
1 **medium onion, chopped**
1 **(20-ounce) can tomatoes**
1 **(16-ounce) can green peas**
2 **bouillon cubes**
¼ **teaspoon saffron threads**
1½ **cups regular rice, uncooked**

Sprinkle chicken with 1 teaspoon salt and paprika. Brown in hot oil in skillet. Remove chicken to 3-quart baking dish with a tight-fitting lid. Add onion to skillet; cook until tender, but not brown. Drain tomatoes and peas, reserving liquid, and add enough water to liquid to make 3 cups. Stir into skillet, scraping brown particles from bottom of pan. Add bouillon cubes, saffron, and remaining ½ teaspoon salt. Bring to a boil. Pour over chicken. Sprinkle rice around chicken; stir so all of rice is moistened. Add tomatoes. Cover tightly. Bake at 350° for 25 minutes. Uncover; toss rice. Add peas; cover and bake 10 minutes. Yield: 6 servings.

BAKED MUSTARD CHICKEN

2 **teaspoons salt**
2 **broiler-fryer chickens, quartered**
½ **cup prepared mustard**
2 **tablespoons vinegar**
2 **tablespoons water**
2 **tablespoons salad oil**
1 **teaspoon dried leaf thyme**
¼ **teaspoon ground ginger**

Sprinkle salt on both sides of chicken. Place skin side up in foil lined shallow baking pan. Combine other ingredients and spoon over chicken. Bake, uncovered, at 375° for 50 to 60 minutes, basting occasionally. Yield: 8 servings.

GLAZED ROAST CHICKEN

1 (3-pound) chicken
Salt
Corn oil
½ cup sherry
⅓ cup dark corn syrup
2 tablespoons melted margarine
2 tablespoons finely chopped onion
½ teaspoon salt
Dash pepper
1½ tablespoons cornstarch
¾ cup water

Clean chicken and rub cavity with salt. Truss. Brush skin with corn oil. Place breast side up on rack in shallow baking pan. Roast at 400° about 1½ hours. Combine sherry, corn syrup, margarine, onion, salt, and pepper; baste chicken with some of sherry mixture after first hour of roasting. Continue roasting, basting frequently and using all the sherry mixture, until chicken is tender, about 30 more minutes. Remove chicken and place on warm platter. Blend cornstarch and water; stir into mixture in pan. Cook over medium heat, stirring constantly, until gravy thickens and boils, about 2 minutes. Slowly spoon over chicken, covering completely. Yield: 4 servings.

ALL-AMERICAN
SWEET-AND-SOUR CHICKEN

2 (2- to 3-pound) broiler-fryer
    chickens, cut up
1 (8-ounce) bottle commercial
    Russian salad dressing
1 (1⅜-ounce) package onion
    soup mix
1 (10-ounce) jar apricot preserves

Place chicken skin side up in large shallow baking dish. Combine Russian dressing, onion soup mix, and preserves; pour over chicken. Bake at 350° 1½ hours, basting occasionally with pan drippings. Yield: 6 to 8 servings.

EAST-WEST CHICKEN

6 large whole chicken breasts, boned
    and butterflied
½ cup commercial teriyaki sauce
½ pound lean ground pork
⅓ cup dry bread crumbs
¼ cup milk
2 tablespoons chopped green onions
    and tops
2 tablespoons chopped water
    chestnuts
2 tablespoons soy sauce
1 egg, slightly beaten
¼ teaspoon ground ginger
⅛ teaspoon white pepper
2 tablespoons melted butter or
    margarine
Hot cooked rice

Place chicken breasts in large plastic bag; add teriyaki sauce. Tie bag and refrigerate 1 hour to allow chicken to marinate.

Combine pork, bread crumbs, milk, green onion, water chestnuts, soy sauce, egg, ginger, and pepper; divide into 6 equal portions. Remove chicken from bag, reserving marinade. Place portion of stuffing mixture on flesh side of each breast. Tuck all ends of breasts over stuffing and secure with poultry skewers. Carefully arrange in baking pan, skin side up.

Blend together butter and 2 tablespoons reserved marinade; brush over chicken. Bake at 350° for 1 hour or until golden brown. Baste frequently with drippings and butter mixture. Serve over hot cooked rice. Yield: 6 servings.

CRISPY CHICKEN

8 chicken legs
8 chicken thighs
8 whole chicken breasts, split
Water
Salt
1 cup mayonnaise
2 cups crushed cornflakes
Salt and pepper

Skin chicken parts, and soak several hours in cold water containing 1 tablespoon salt per 2 quarts water. Drain and pat chicken pieces dry with paper towels. Coat chicken well with mayonnaise; roll in cornflake crumbs.

Place the pieces an inch apart on a baking sheet; sprinkle generously with salt and pepper. Bake at 325° for 1 hour and 15 minutes. Yield: 10 to 12 servings.

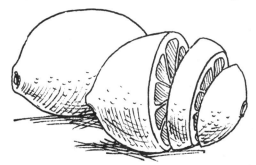

CHICKEN MARENGO

1 (2½- to 3½-pound) broiler-fryer
    chicken, cut up
½ teaspoon salt
¼ teaspoon pepper
¼ cup all-purpose flour
⅓ cup corn oil
2 onions, thinly sliced
1 clove garlic
¼ pound mushrooms, slices
3 tablespoons all-purpose flour
1 (20-ounce) can tomatoes
½ cup water
¼ cup sherry

Sprinkle chicken with salt and pepper, lightly coat with flour. Heat oil in a heavy skillet; add chicken and brown lightly on all sides. Remove chicken and place in a 2-quart casserole. Add onion, garlic, and mushrooms to drippings in skillet; cook until tender. (Add more oil if needed.) Remove from heat; remove garlic. Add flour (use any leftover flour from coating chicken) and mix well. Add tomatoes and water; cook, stirring constantly until mixture comes to a boil and is slightly thickened. Add sherry. Pour over chicken. Cover and bake at 350° about 45 minutes. Yield: 4 servings.

OVEN BARBECUED CHICKEN

1 (3- to 3½-pound) broiler chicken
    All-purpose flour
¼ cup salad oil
1 onion, chopped
2 tablespoons vinegar
2 tablespoons firmly packed brown
    sugar
¼ cup lemon juice
1 cup catsup
3 tablespoons Worcestershire sauce
½ tablespoon prepared mustard
1 cup water
½ cup chopped celery
    Salt
    Dash cayenne

Cut chicken into serving pieces; dredge in flour and brown in hot oil. Remove chicken; drain off excess drippings. Brown onion in remaining drippings; add remaining ingredients and simmer 30 minutes. Pour over chicken. Bake uncovered at 325° about 1 hour or until tender. Yield: 4 servings.

PARTY-SPECIAL CHICKEN

2 pounds chicken pieces
2 cups diagonally sliced celery
    (1 inch)
½ cup chopped onion
½ teaspoon ground ginger
2 tablespoons butter or margarine
1 (10¾-ounce) can condensed cream
    of chicken soup
1 (11-ounce) can mandarin oranges,
    drained
¼ cup flaked coconut

Brown chicken and sauté celery, onion, and ginger in butter in heavy skillet until vegetables are tender. Remove chicken and place, skin side down, in shallow baking dish. Stir soup into skillet to loosen brown bits; pour over chicken. Bake at 375° for 30 minutes. Turn chicken; bake 30 minutes longer. Top with oranges and coconut during last 10 minutes of cooking time. Yield: 4 servings.

CONTINENTAL CHICKEN

1 (3-pound) broiler-fryer chicken,
  cut into pieces
⅓ cup seasoned all-purpose flour
¼ cup melted butter
1 (10¾-ounce) can condensed cream
  of chicken soup
2½ tablespoons grated onion
1 teaspoon salt
  Dash pepper
1 tablespoon chopped parsley
½ teaspoon celery flakes
½ teaspoon ground dried thyme
1⅓ cups water
1⅓ cups precooked rice

Dredge chicken in flour; brown in butter.
Remove chicken. Combine soup, onion,
seasonings, and water with drippings;
cook and stir until mixture boils. Spread
rice in 1½-quart shallow casserole. Pour
all but ⅓ cup soup mixture over rice. Stir
to moisten. Top with chicken and
remaining soup mixture. Cover; bake at
375° for 30 minutes. Yield: 4 servings.

BAKED CHICKEN WITH GRAPES

1 (4- to 4½-pound) roasting chicken
1½ teaspoons salt
½ teaspoon pepper
¼ teaspoon garlic salt
½ teaspoon ground ginger
  Grape Stuffing
½ cup butter, softened, divided
½ cup dry white wine
1 cup chicken broth
2 cups seedless grapes
1 tablespoon all-purpose flour
½ cup orange juice
  Salt and pepper to taste

Prepare chicken for roasting. Rub cavity
with half of combined dry seasonings.
Stuff with Grape Stuffing and truss. Rub
outside of bird with half the softened
butter; sprinkle with remaining
seasonings. Put the remaining butter in
a roasting pan with a roasting rack.
Place bird, breast side down, on rack.

Bake at 425° for 30 minutes. Turn bird;
reduce heat to 325°. Baste and bake 45
minutes longer or until legs move freely
in sockets and meat is fork tender.
Remove chicken to a warm platter.

Remove the roasting pan to top of
stove and place over medium heat.
Remove rack. Stir in wine; simmer
several minutes while stirring bits of
scrapings from the bottom of pan. Add
broth; simmer 5 minutes. Pour this sauce
into a saucepan and stir in grapes.
Combine flour and orange juice; add to
sauce. Return sauce to medium heat;
simmer until slightly thickened. Season
with salt and pepper. Keep sauce warm
and serve over chicken. Yield: 6 servings.

Grape Stuffing:

3 tablespoons minced onion
¼ cup melted butter
2 cups coarse bread crumbs or
  croutons
½ cup chicken broth or consommé
1½ teaspoons poultry seasoning
¼ teaspoon dried tarragon leaves,
  crumbled
½ teaspoon salt
  Pepper to taste
1 cup seedless grapes

Sauté onion in butter until tender. Stir
in remaining ingredients and blend well.
Yield: about 3 cups.

SESAME CHICKEN

2 (2½-pound) fryers, quartered
¼ cup sesame seeds
⅓ cup corn oil
2 tablespoons finely chopped
  onion
½ clove garlic, finely chopped
1 teaspoon salt
½ teaspoon ground cardamom
½ teaspoon ground ginger
  Dash cloves
  Dash chili powder
  Sesame Sauce

Place chicken skin side down in shallow baking pan. Combine remaining ingredients; brush chicken with mixture, reserving some for basting. Bake at 375° for 30 minutes, basting frequently. Turn skin side up; continue baking and basting about 30 minutes or until chicken is tender. Serve with Sesame Sauce. Yield: 8 servings.

Sesame Sauce:

    Pan drippings from Sesame
        Chicken
1 tablespoon cornstarch
1 cup water
    Basting mixture from Sesame
        Chicken

Remove chicken pieces from baking pan. Blend cornstarch with water; stir into pan gravy. Add remaining basting mixture. Cook over low heat, stirring constantly, until sauce comes to boil and boils 2 minutes. Yield: about ¾ cup.

ONIONS STUFFED WITH CHICKEN LIVERS

4 large Bermuda onions
2 teaspoons butter, melted
1 tablespoon soft bread crumbs
6 chicken livers, broiled and chopped
    Salt to taste
    Finely rolled bread or cracker
        crumbs
    Butter

Boil onions, without removing outside skins, in salted water until tender. Drain, peel, and scoop out enough of the centers to leave a cavity the size of a small egg. Chop half the quantity of scooped-out onion and combine with melted butter, 1 tablespoon soft bread crumbs, coarsely chopped chicken livers, and salt. Mix thoroughly. Stuff onions, sprinkle lightly with finely rolled bread crumbs, and dot with additional butter. Bake in 400° oven until brown. Yield: 4 servings.

SPANISH CHICKEN AND RICE

1 (3-pound) broiler-fryer chicken, cut
    into serving pieces
    Salt and pepper
    All-purpose flour
3 tablespoons salad oil
1 large onion, chopped
1 green pepper, chopped
1 (4-ounce) can mushrooms
1 cup regular rice, uncooked
1 (16-ounce) can tomatoes
1 (4-ounce) can tomato sauce
1 (10¾-ounce) can condensed
    mushroom soup
1 clove garlic, minced

Season chicken with salt and pepper and dredge in flour. Brown chicken lightly in hot oil. Remove chicken from oil and place in a 2-quart casserole.

Sauté onion and green pepper in hot oil about 10 minutes; add mushrooms and cook an additional 10 minutes. Add rice, tomatoes, tomato sauce, mushroom soup, and garlic to onion-pepper mixture; cook about 15 minutes. If mixture seems too dry, add hot water at this stage. Pour mixture over chicken; cover, and cook at 325° about 1 hour or until rice is done. Yield: 6 servings.

LEMON CHICKEN

4 selected pieces of
    frying-size chicken
½ teaspoon salt
¾ teaspoon pepper
¼ cup salad oil
1 small clove garlic
1 teaspoon salt
2 teaspoons chopped onion
½ teaspoon ground dried thyme
½ cup lemon juice

Season chicken with salt and pepper. Place oil in skillet and brown chicken. Mash garlic with salt and add the remaining ingredients, mixing well. Pour this mixture over the browned chicken. Cover and cook at 325° for 40 minutes. Yield: 2 servings.

POULET ELEGANT

1 (9-ounce) package frozen artichoke
    hearts
12 small new potatoes, peeled
3 whole chicken breasts, halved
¼ cup all-purpose flour
½ cup butter
2 tablespoons chopped green onion
1 (6-ounce) jar mushrooms,
    undrained
¼ cup dry red wine
½ teaspoon seasoned salt
¼ teaspoon seasoned pepper
½ cup commercial sour cream
1 tablespoon all-purpose flour

Thaw artichoke hearts. Arrange in
buttered 2½-quart casserole with
potatoes. Coat chicken pieces with ¼ cup
flour. Brown carefully in butter. Place on
top of vegetables in casserole. Cook green
onion until tender in same skillet used
for browning chicken. Add mushrooms
and wine. Pour over chicken.

Sprinkle with salt and pepper. Cover.
Bake at 350° for 1½ hours.

Remove chicken and vegetables to
warm serving platter. Blend together
sour cream and 1 tablespoon flour. Add to
juices in casserole. Heat this gravy
through and serve with chicken. Yield: 6
servings.

CHICKEN À LA CHASE

1 (2½- to 3-pound) broiler chicken, cut
    into serving-size pieces
    Garlic powder
1 (10¾-ounce) can condensed cream
    of mushroom soup
1 pint whipping cream
2 ounces sherry
    Paprika
    Dash each ground dried basil,
      marjoram, thyme, and tarragon
    Chopped parsley
    Chopped mushrooms (optional)

Put chicken in a shallow roasting pan
and cover generously with garlic powder.

Combine mushroom soup, cream, and
sherry. Spread chicken very generously
with paprika; then add basil, marjoram,
thyme, and tarragon. Pour mushroom
sauce over chicken, and sprinkle with
chopped parsley. Cover pan and bake at
350° for 1½ hours. Chopped mushrooms
may be added the last 15 minutes of
baking time, if desired. Yield: 4 to 6
servings.

SESAME-HERB CHICKEN BREASTS

¼ cup butter, melted
2 tablespoons grated Parmesan
    cheese
½ teaspoon salt
⅛ teaspoon pepper
⅛ teaspoon thyme leaves, crumbled
2 large whole chicken breasts, split
2 tablespoons sesame seeds

Combine butter, Parmesan cheese, salt,
pepper, and thyme; dip each chicken
breast in butter mixture; place skin side
up in casserole. Cover securely with
aluminum foil. Place under broiler about
4 inches from heat about 15 minutes.
Turn chicken, cover with foil, and cook
10 minutes on other side.

Add sesame seeds to remaining butter
mixture. Remove foil and spread a
spoonful of the sesame seed mixture on
top of each breast. Return to broiler for 3
to 5 minutes or until sesame seeds are
browned. Serve with pan juices. Yield: 2
servings.

LEMON BARBECUED CHICKEN

2 (1½- to 2½-pound) broiler-fryer
    chickens
1 small clove garlic
½ teaspoon salt
¼ cup salad oil
½ cup lemon juice
2 tablespoons chopped onion
½ teaspoon pepper
½ teaspoon thyme

Split chickens in half lengthwise with backbone, necks, and breast bones removed. Mash garlic with salt; stir in remaining ingredients. Brush chickens with sauce and place skin side down in broiler pan. Place under broiler so that surface of chickens is 6 to 8 inches below broiling unit. Broil for 20 to 25 minutes or until brown, basting occasionally with lemon sauce. Turn; brush with sauce; continue broiling and basting for 15 to 20 minutes or until done. Yield: 4 servings.

GLAZED CHICKEN WINGS

1 teaspoon salt, divided
¾ teaspoon pepper, divided
¼ cup all-purpose flour
3 pounds chicken wings
½ cup melted margarine
1 (10½-ounce) can condensed beef
    broth
1 (12-ounce) jar apricot or peach
    preserves
⅓ cup Dijon mustard
5 tablespoons firmly packed brown
    sugar
2 tablespoons honey
1 cup wild rice, uncooked
1 cup regular rice, uncooked
1 (29-ounce) can sliced peaches,
    drained
1 (17-ounce) can apricot halves,
    drained

Combine ½ teaspoon salt, ½ teaspoon pepper, and flour. Dredge chicken wings in flour mixture; brown on both sides in margarine in a Dutch oven. Add beef broth; cover and cook 15 to 20 minutes or until tender.

To make glaze, combine remaining salt and pepper, preserves, mustard, sugar, and honey in a saucepan; heat.

Drain chicken wings; place on a cookie sheet or broiler pan. Brush with glaze; broil until well browned and bubbly. Turn on other side and brush with glaze; broil.

Cook wild rice and regular rice as directed on each package; combine. Spoon onto a hot platter; arrange chicken on top. Garnish with part of peaches and apricots. Warm remaining glaze; spoon over chicken wings. Serve remaining fruit as a side dish. Yield: 8 to 10 servings.

BARBECUED CHICKEN

3 broiler-fryer chickens, halved
    Melted butter
    Barbecue Sauce

Allow ½ chicken per person. Place chicken halves on broiling rack, skin side down, about 5 inches from the heat. Broil for a few minutes, turn, brush with melted butter, and broil other side for same length of time. Turn chicken pieces at regular intervals, allowing 45 minutes to 1 hour cooking time. Baste frequently with Barbecue Sauce. Yield: 6 servings.

Barbecue Sauce:

½ cup vinegar
⅓ cup salad oil
1 teaspoon Worcestershire sauce
½ teaspoon grated onion
½ clove garlic, minced
¾ teaspoon salt
¼ teaspoon paprika
1½ tablespoons tomato paste
    Few drops hot sauce
¼ teaspoon dry mustard

Combine all ingredients and use as a baste for broiling chicken. Yield: about 1 cup.

SUNNY ORANGE-GLAZED CHICKEN

1 cup orange juice
1 tablespoon grated orange rind
1 cup firmly packed brown sugar
2 tablespoons melted butter or
    margarine
1 teaspoon dry mustard
¼ teaspoon ground allspice
1 (3½- to 4-pound) chicken,
    quartered
1 orange, sliced

Combine orange juice and rind, brown sugar, butter, dry mustard, and allspice. Place chicken on rack in shallow baking pan. Top with orange slices; pour glaze over chicken and oranges. Bake at 375° for 1 hour, basting frequently, until chicken is glazed and well browned. Yield: 4 servings.

CHICKEN BREASTS BRAZILIA

4 whole chicken breasts (about 6 or 7
    ounces each), boned
1 (14-ounce) can hearts of palm,
    drained
    Melted butter
    Salt and white pepper
    Hollandaise Sauce
    Chopped chives

Wrap chicken breasts around stalks of palm heart and secure with a wooden pick. Place seam side down in a buttered pan and cover breasts generously with melted butter and season with salt and white pepper. Bake at 400° for 25 minutes. Top with Hollandaise Sauce; sprinkle with chopped chives. Yield: 4 servings.

Hollandaise Sauce:

5 egg yolks
    Juice of 1 lemon
    Dash hot sauce
    Salt to taste
½ cup melted butter

Combine egg yolks, lemon juice, hot sauce, and salt in container of electric blender; process on high speed until well blended. Gradually add melted butter and continue to blend. Yield: about 1 cup.

DIETER'S CHICKEN BROIL

1 broiler-fryer chicken, cut into
    serving-size pieces
¼ cup grapefruit juice
1 teaspoon seasoned salt
1 teaspoon seasoned pepper
⅓ cup corn oil

Place chicken in large bowl. Combine remaining ingredients and pour over chicken. Cover and marinate overnight in refrigerator, turning once or twice, if convenient. Drain chicken, reserving marinade. Place chicken on rack set 3 to 6 inches from heat in gas range or 6 to 9 inches from medium broil heat (lower rack if oven has only one broiling temperature) in electric range. Broil for 20 minutes, basting occasionally with reserved marinade. Turn and broil, continuing to base, about 15 more minutes or until done. Yield: 4 servings.

SHERRIED BREAST OF CHICKEN

2 whole chicken breasts, halved
1½ tablespoons all-purpose flour
½ teaspoon salt
    Oil for frying
2 tablespoons all-purpose flour
½ cup chicken broth
1 cup half-and-half
1 egg yolk, slightly beaten
2 tablespoons sherry
    Toasted bread

Dip chicken breasts in seasoned flour; fry in oil until tender and browned. Remove to serving dish, add 2 tablespoons flour to skillet, and stir until well blended. Add broth and half-and-half, stirring until thickened. Add egg yolk and sherry just before serving. Pour over chicken breasts. Serve on toast. Yield: 2 servings.

CHICKEN SCALLOPINI

8 broiler-fryer chicken thighs, boned
1 teaspoon salt
2 tablespoons butter or margarine
1 tablespoon lemon juice
2 tablespoons chopped parsley
1 tablespoon chopped chives or
    green onions
¼ teaspoon dried leaf marjoram

Place chicken between 2 pieces of aluminum foil; pound with meat mallet or rolling pin to flatten. Sprinkle with salt. Melt butter over medium heat in large skillet. Add chicken, skin side down; sauté about 10 minutes or until lightly browned. Turn chicken, and sprinkle with lemon juice and herbs; continue cooking until tender. Serve hot. Yield: 4 servings.

CHICKEN CROQUETTES

1 (4- to 5-pound) hen
½ cup butter or margarine
2 tablespoons all-purpose flour
2 cups half-and-half
    Salt and pepper to taste
1 (10¾-ounce) can condensed cream
    of mushroom soup
1 cup chopped mushrooms
    Bread crumbs
3 or 4 eggs, well beaten
    Oil for frying

Cook chicken in boiling water until tender; cool. Bone and chop coarsely.

Melt butter; add flour and blend well. Add half-and-half; cook over medium heat until thick, stirring constantly. Season to taste. Remove from heat. Add mushroom soup, chicken, and mushrooms; mix well. Chill overnight.

Drop chicken mixture by teaspoonfuls onto waxed paper covered with bread crumbs. Shape into 3- × 1½-inch logs; roll in bread crumbs. Dip croquettes in beaten eggs; quickly roll again in bread crumbs. Refrigerate until ready to use. Drop into deep hot oil and fry until brown. Yield: about 3½ dozen croquettes.

TEMPURA FRIED CHICKEN

4 whole chicken breasts, halved and
    boned
1 egg
    Milk
½ cup tempura batter mix
½ teaspoon salt
¼ teaspoon pepper
½ cup peanut oil

Cut each half of chicken breast into 4 strips. Break egg into measuring cup; add enough milk to make ½ cup. Stir egg and milk into tempura batter mix; add salt and pepper. Dip chicken into batter; brown in hot oil in tempura pan. Yield: 4 to 6 servings.

Note: When frying chicken, leave a few strips of chicken in pan before adding additional strips; the chicken left in the pan will absorb the heat of the oil and keep it from overheating.

FRIED CHICKEN

1 teaspoon paprika
1 teaspoon salt
½ teaspoon pepper
1 cup all-purpose flour
6 whole chicken breasts (or 1 fryer
    cut into pieces)
2 eggs, beaten
    Oil for frying

Combine dry ingredients in a paper bag. Dip each piece of chicken in egg and then shake it thoroughly in the bag of dry ingredients. Fry in very hot oil about 12 minutes on each side. Yield: 6 servings.

ROLLED CHICKEN ELEGANTE

    1 (3-ounce) can chopped
        mushrooms, drained
    2 tablespoons melted margarine
    2 tablespoons all-purpose flour
    ½ cup half-and-half
    ¼ teaspoon salt
        Dash cayenne pepper
 1¼ cups shredded sharp Cheddar
        cheese
    6 or 7 whole chicken breasts,
        boned
        Salt
        All-purpose flour
    2 eggs, slightly beaten
    ¾ cup fine, dry bread crumbs
        Oil for frying

Sauté mushrooms in margarine about 5 minutes. Blend in flour; stir in half-and-half. Add salt and cayenne; cook and stir until mixture becomes very thick. Stir in cheese; cook over very low heat, stirring constantly, until cheese is melted. Turn mixture into a 9-inch pie plate. Cover; chill thoroughly, about 1 hour. Cut the firm cheese mixture into 6 or 7 equal portions; shape into short sticks.

Remove skin from chicken breasts. To make cutlets, place each piece of chicken, boned side up, between two pieces of plastic wrap. (Overlap where chicken breast is split.) Working from the center, pound with wooden mallet to form cutlets not quite ¼ inch thick. Peel off plastic wrap. Sprinkle meat with salt.

Place a cheese stick on each chicken breast. Tucking in the sides, roll chicken jelly roll fashion. Press to seal well.

Dust chicken rolls with flour, dip in egg, then roll in bread crumbs. Cover and chill chicken rolls thoroughly, at least 1 hour. (Or prepare ahead when entertaining; the rolls can chill all afternoon or overnight.) About an hour before serving, fry rolls in deep, hot oil for 5 minutes or until crisp and golden brown; drain on paper towels. Place rolls in shallow baking dish and bake at 325° about 30 to 45 minutes. Yield: 6 to 7 servings.

GOLDEN CRISP CHICKEN

    2 (2½-pound) broiler-fryer chickens,
        cut into serving-size pieces
    2 cups water
    ½ cup honey
    ½ cup soy sauce
    ¼ cup vinegar
    1 tablespoon molasses
    2 tablespoons water
    ¾ cup all-purpose flour
    1 tablespoon salt
    1 quart salad oil

Wash and dry chicken. Place chicken in large skillet with 2 cups water and cover tightly. Bring to boil, then reduce heat and simmer, covered, for 45 minutes or until tender. Drain; rinse in cold water and dry with paper towels. Combine honey, soy sauce, vinegar, molasses, and 2 tablespoons water; brush over chicken. Let stand about 5 minutes, then brush again with honey mixture. Coat chicken pieces with combined flour and salt. Slowly heat oil to 375° in deep pan. Fry a few pieces at a time for 2 to 3 minutes or until golden brown. Drain on paper towels. Serve at once. Yield: 6 servings.

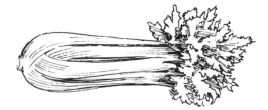

BONELESS BREASTS OF CAPON

  16 (8-ounce) whole boneless breasts
        of capon or chicken breasts
        Salt
        Butter
        Herb Stuffing
    ½ pound melted butter
    1 quart water
    1 cup Rhine wine
        Peach halves, mandarin orange
        sections, and parsley

Thoroughly wash and pat dry capon or chicken pieces. Salt, using about ¼ teaspoon salt for each piece. Butter breasts generously inside and out and stuff lightly with Herb Stuffing; truss securely. Place breasts on rack in a shallow pan to which the butter, water, and Rhine wine have been added. Roast uncovered at 400° until brown, about 20 to 25 minutes. Reduce heat to 350°. Cover tightly and continue roasting until tender. The entire cooking time will be about 1 hour.

Uncover during the last 20 minutes and baste several times with pan drippings. Place on a serving platter and garnish with peach halves, mandarin orange sections, and parsley. Yield: 16 servings.

Herb Stuffing:

  3 tablespoons minced onion
  1 cup chopped celery
  ¼ cup melted butter
3½ cups white bread crumbs
3½ cups corn bread crumbs
  2 teaspoons salt
  ½ teaspoon pepper
  ½ teaspoon savory
  2 or 3 teaspoons ground dried sage
  1 egg, slightly beaten
  ½ cup milk
  2 cups hot chicken broth

Saute onion and celery in butter; add to crumbs. Add remaining ingredients and mix well. If dressing seems too dry, add more broth. Lightly stuff breasts. Any leftover stuffing may be baked in a shallow pan at 400° for 15 to 25 minutes. Yield: about 2½ quarts.

CRUNCHY FRIED CHICKEN

1 (2½- to 3-pound) broiler-fryer
    chicken
  Seasoned salt
  Seasoned pepper
1 teaspoon dried oregano
1 to 1½ cups buttermilk
  All-purpose flour
  Oil for frying

Cut chicken into serving-size pieces; season generously with seasoned salt and pepper. Stir oregano into buttermilk. Dip chicken pieces in buttermilk, coating thoroughly. Roll chicken in flour. Deep fry in hot oil until golden brown and crunchy. Yield: 4 to 6 servings.

CHICKEN FRIED RICE

  1 cup diced cooked chicken
  ½ teaspoon salt
  1 tablespoon soy sauce
  ⅓ cup corn oil
  2 cups regular rice, uncooked
2½ cups chicken broth or bouillon
  ½ cup chopped onion
  ½ cup thinly sliced celery
  ¼ cup minced green pepper
  2 eggs, slightly beaten
  ½ cup finely shredded Chinese
     cabbage or lettuce

Combine chicken, salt, and soy sauce; let stand 15 minutes. Heat corn oil in skillet over medium heat or in electric skillet set at 350°. Add rice. Fry, stirring frequently, until golden brown. Reduce heat to simmer. Gradually add chicken mixture and broth. Cover; cook 15 to 25 minutes or until rice is almost tender.

Remove cover the last few minutes of cooking. Increase heat to moderate, and add onion, celery, and green pepper. Cook, uncovered, a few minutes, until liquid is absorbed. Push rice to sides of pan. Add eggs and cook until almost set; then mix into rice mixture. Stir in cabbage. Serve immediately. Yield: 6 to 8 servings.

CHICKEN LIVERS VASSILAKOS

5 slices bacon, cut into pieces
3 tablespoons salad oil
½ teaspoon salt
⅓ cup all-purpose flour
½ teaspoon dried oregano
1 pound chicken livers, halved

Fry bacon bits until almost done. Discard bacon drippings; put oil in skillet with bacon, and heat to medium.

Combine salt, flour, and oregano in a paper bag. Shake chicken livers in this mixture. Fry livers and bacon about 10 minutes, stirring occasionally. Liver is done when brown on the outside and slightly pink inside. If in doubt, check by cutting one piece open with knife. Yield: 3 to 4 servings.

OVEN-FRIED CHICKEN

1 cup all-purpose flour
2 teaspoons salt
¼ teaspoon pepper
2 teaspoons paprika
½ cup salad oil
1 (2½- to 3-pound) fryer chicken, cut up

Combine flour, salt, pepper, and paprika in paper bag. Put oil in a 13- × 9- × 2-inch pan and set in 425° oven to heat. Shake 3 or 4 pieces of chicken at a time in bag to coat thoroughly. Place chicken skin side down in single layer in hot oil. Bake at 425° for 30 minutes. Turn skin side up and bake another 30 minutes or until chicken is tender. Yield: 4 servings.

SPICED CHICKEN

1 cup orange juice
1½ cups sliced peaches
2 tablespoons firmly packed brown sugar
2 tablespoons vinegar
1 teaspoon ground mace or nutmeg
1 teaspoon basil
1 clove garlic, minced
6 chicken legs
6 chicken thighs
½ cup all-purpose flour
1 teaspoon salt
    Dash pepper
    Salad oil

Combine first 7 ingredients in saucepan; cook slowly for 10 minutes.

Dredge chicken pieces in mixture of flour, salt, and pepper. Pour salad oil to depth of 1 inch in skillet; heat. Brown chicken pieces in hot oil. Remove chicken and drain off all except 2 tablespoons oil in skillet.

Put chicken back in skillet; pour fruit sauce over top. Cover and simmer for 20 minutes. Yield: 4 to 6 servings.

HOME-STYLE FRIED CHICKEN

½ cup all-purpose flour
1 teaspoon salt
½ teaspoon paprika
¼ teaspoon pepper
1 (2½- to 3½-pound) broiler-fryer chicken, cut up
¼ cup corn oil

Combine flour, salt, paprika, and pepper. Coat chicken pieces with mixture; shake off excess. Heat oil in large heavy skillet over medium heat about 3 minutes. Carefully add chicken and fry, turning once, for 15 minutes or until golden brown. Cover and cook over low heat 20 minutes longer. Remove cover and cook until chicken is tender and coating is crisp. Yield: 4 servings.

CRISPY FRIED CHICKEN

2 broiler-fryer chickens, cut into
   serving-size pieces
2 teaspoons Ac'cent
⅔ cup evaporated milk
1¼ cups all-purpose flour
1½ teaspoons salt
½ teaspoon paprika
⅛ teaspoon pepper
   Oil for frying

Wash and dry chicken; sprinkle with
Ac'cent, and let stand 15 minutes.
Pour evaporated milk into bowl.
Combine flour, salt, paprika, and pepper.
Dip chicken pieces in evaporated milk;
roll in flour mixture.
Pour oil into skillet to a depth of 1
inch; heat until drop of water sizzles in
oil. Fry chicken, uncovered, for 15 to 20
minutes on each side, turning only once.
Drain well on absorbent paper. Yield: 8
servings.

SAVORY ORANGE FRIED CHICKEN

1 (2½- to 3-pound) broiler-fryer
   chicken, cut into serving-size
   pieces
4 teaspoons grated orange peel,
   divided
¾ cup orange juice
½ teaspoon salt
½ teaspoon ground ginger
⅛ teaspoon pepper
¾ cup all-purpose flour
1½ teaspoons paprika
1½ teaspoons salt
½ cup shortening

Place cut chicken in shallow dish or
heavy plastic bag. Combine 2 teaspoons
orange peel, orange juice, ½ teaspoon
salt, ginger, and pepper. Pour over
chicken; marinate in refrigerator for 2 to
3 hours. Drain, reserve marinade.
Combine remaining orange peel, flour,
paprika, and 1½ teaspoons salt in a

paper bag; shake chicken pieces, a few at
a time, in bag until well coated. Save
flour mixture for gravy.
Heat shortening in heavy skillet;
brown chicken, turning to brown evenly.
Cover tightly, reduce heat, and cook
slowly until chicken is tender, about 40
minutes. Uncover and continue cooking
about 10 minutes to "recrisp" coating.
Remove to warm serving platter. Add
water to marinade to yield 1½ cups. Pour
off all but 3 tablespoons drippings from
skillet; add 3 tablespoons reserved flour
mixture and cook until mixture is smooth
and bubbling. Add marinade and cook,
stirring constantly, until thickened.
Serve with chicken. Yield: 4 servings.

BARBECUED CHICKEN DELIGHT

2 (2-pound) broiler chickens
   Salad oil
⅓ cup cider vinegar
1 teaspoon Worcestershire sauce
½ teaspoon onion salt
¼ teaspoon garlic salt
½ teaspoon salt
⅛ teaspoon pepper
   Dash paprika
1 tablespoon tomato paste
½ cup salad oil

Split chickens in half; brush with oil and
place skin side down on grill about 5
inches from heat. Grill about 15 minutes,
turn, brush with oil, and and grill on the
other side. Turn skin side down again,
and continue to grill. Allow 45 to 60
minutes for grilling chicken. Combine
remaining ingredients to make a sauce;
baste chicken frequently while grilling.
Yield: 4 servings.
Variation: Combine 5 tablespoons
salad oil, 2 tablespoons vinegar, ½
teaspoon dry mustard, and ½ teaspoon
Worcestershire sauce. Use instead of
sauce given above.

BREEZY BARBECUED CHICKEN

1 cup salad oil
⅓ cup white vinegar
3 tablespoons sugar
3 tablespoons catsup
1 tablespoon grated onion
1½ teaspoons salt
1 teaspoon dry mustard
1 tablespoon Worcestershire sauce
1 clove garlic, minced
　Dash hot sauce
3 (2-pound) broiler-size chickens,
　halved

Combine first 10 ingredients, and mix well; add chicken, and marinate in refrigerator overnight. Grill chicken over medium heat about 45 minutes, turning often and basting frequently with marinade. Yield: 6 servings.

SAVORY BARBECUED CHICKEN

½ cup soy sauce
½ cup firmly packed brown
　sugar
3 drops hot sauce
1½ teaspoons ground ginger
½ teaspoon Ac'cent
½ teaspoon paprika
1 clove garlic, chopped
1 cup pineapple juice
¼ cup melted butter
½ cup water
2 or 3 broiler-fryer chickens,
　halved

Combine all ingredients except chicken. Cut chickens in half and marinate in sauce mixture for 3 hours, turning every 30 minutes. Grill chicken over medium heat about 45 minutes, turning often and basting frequently with marinade. Yield: 4 to 6 servings.

CHICKEN KIEV

1 cup butter, softened
2 tablespoons chopped parsley
1 teaspoon rosemary
¾ teaspoon salt
⅛ teaspoon pepper
6 whole chicken breasts, split,
　boned, and skinned
¾ cup all-purpose flour
3 eggs, well beaten
1½ to 2 cups bread crumbs
　Oil for frying

Combine butter and seasonings in a small bowl; blend thoroughly. Shape butter mixture into 2 sticks; cover and put in freezer about 45 minutes or until firm.

Place each half of chicken breast on a sheet of waxed paper; flatten to ¼-inch thickness using a meat mallet or rolling pin.

Cut each stick of butter mixture into 6 pats; place a pat in center of each half of chicken breast. Fold long sides of chicken over butter; fold ends over and secure with wooden pick. Dredge each piece of chicken in flour, dip in egg, and coat with bread crumbs. Cover and refrigerate about 1 hour.

Fry chicken in salad oil heated to 350°. Cook 5 minutes on each side or until browned, turning with tongs. Place in warm oven until all chicken is fried. Yield: 12 servings.

BARBECUED CHICKEN DELUXE

½ cup dry white wine
½ cup salad oil
1 teaspoon chopped chives
2 tablespoons chopped
　parsley
3 (2-pound) chickens, cut up
　Tomato Wine Sauce

Combine wine, salad oil, chives, and parsley; marinate chicken at room temperature for 1 hour in this mixture. Turn chicken in marinade several times.

Broil or grill for 30 minutes or until done, turning frequently and basting with Tomato Wine Sauce. Yield: 8 servings.

Tomato Wine Sauce:

1 cup canned tomatoes
1 cup dry white wine
1 cup thinly sliced okra
1½ cups beef bouillon
½ cup finely chopped celery
1 tablespoon lemon juice
¼ teaspoon hot sauce
2 cloves garlic, minced
1 teaspoon salt
1 teaspoon chili powder
¼ cup Worcestershire sauce
½ cup salad oil
1 tablespoon sugar
1 bay leaf, crumbled
½ teaspoon dried oregano
½ teaspoon dried basil
½ cup finely chopped onion
   Freshly ground black pepper

Combine all ingredients and bring to a boil. Reduce heat and simmer 45 minutes. Strain or put through blender. Serve with barbecued chicken. This sauce is also excellent with ham, pork, or lamb. Yield: about 6 cups.

BARBECUED CHICKEN BREASTS

2 whole chicken breasts, halved
1 clove garlic, crushed
¼ cup olive oil
½ teaspoon thyme
½ teaspoon dry mustard
¼ cup wine vinegar

Clean and wash chicken breasts; set aside. Combine garlic, olive oil, thyme, mustard, and vinegar to make a basting sauce. Place chicken breasts on grill over medium heat. Cook about 10 minutes on each side before beginning to baste with sauce. Continue cooking, basting, and turning chicken until done, about 30 minutes. Yield: 4 servings.

PEPPERY BARBECUED CHICKEN

1 cup salad oil
2 cups lemon juice or vinegar
1 cup water
3 to 4 tablespoons white pepper
2 to 3 (2½-pound) broiler-fryer
   chickens, cut up

Combine salad oil, lemon juice, water, and pepper in a large flat dish. Lay chicken pieces in marinade and refrigerate for 2 hours. Remove chicken from marinade and drain carefully. Place in hinged basket on grill over low heat; cook until meat is done, brushing often with marinade, and turn basket often to keep chicken from burning. Chicken should cook about 25 minutes. Yield: 6 to 8 servings.

LEMONY GRILLED CHICKEN

2 (2½- to 3-pound) broiler-fryer
   chickens
1 cup salad oil
½ cup lemon juice
1 tablespoon salt
1 teaspoon paprika
2 teaspoons crushed dried basil
2 teaspoons onion powder
½ teaspoon crushed dried
   thyme
½ teaspoon garlic powder

Split chickens in halves or quarters; place in shallow baking pans. Combine other ingredients in a jar and shake well to blend. Pour sauce over chicken; cover tightly and marinate in refrigerator for 6 to 8 hours or overnight, turning chicken occasionally.
   Remove chicken from refrigerator about an hour before grilling. Place chicken on grill, skin side up, and cook about 20 to 25 minutes, brushing often with sauce. Turn chicken and cook an additional 20 minutes.
   Chicken may also be cooked in oven. Place 8 inches from broiler; brush often with sauce. Yield: 4 to 8 servings.

BARBECUED ORIENTAL CHICKEN

1 cup soy sauce
1 cup grapefruit juice
1 teaspoon sugar
½ teaspoon ground ginger
1 (2½- to 3½-pound) broiler-fryer
    chicken, cut up, or
    8 drumsticks
¼ cup corn oil or melted
    margarine

Combine soy sauce, grapefruit juice, sugar, and ginger in a large shallow dish. Add chicken pieces, turning to coat both sides. Cover and marinate in refrigerator several hours or overnight, turning occasionally. Remove chicken from marinade and brush with corn oil or margarine. Grill about 6 inches from the source of heat, brushing with marinade and turning frequently. Grill 45 to 60 minutes or until tender and brown. Yield: 4 servings.

CITRUS-HONEY BARBECUED CHICKEN

2 (2- to 2½-pound) broiler-fryer
    chickens, quartered,
    or halved
½ cup lemon juice
½ cup orange juice
⅓ cup honey
1 cup salad oil
2 tablespoons prepared mustard
½ teaspoon dried thyme
½ teaspoon dried marjoram

Cut away back bone from chicken halves or quarters; place chicken in shallow glass dish. Combine remaining ingredients in covered jar; shake to blend well. Pour over chicken; marinate in refrigerator for several hours, turning occasionally. Drain chicken, reserving marinade. Place cut side down on grill over medium coals. Cook slowly, 25 to 30 minutes on each side, until tender. Baste occasionally with reserved marinade. Yield: 4 to 6 servings.

MEDITERRANEAN CHICKEN

½ cup olive oil
½ cup white wine
¼ cup honey
¼ cup white wine vinegar
2 teaspoons garlic salt
½ teaspoon ground oregano
2 (2-pound) broiler-fryer chickens
1 lemon, thinly sliced
1 orange, thinly sliced

Combine oil, wine, honey, vinegar, garlic salt, and oregano; blend well. Pour over chickens; marinate in refrigerator overnight. (Turn occasionally, if possible.)

Center chickens securely on spit of rotisserie. Cook over low heat for 1 hour or until chicken is tender and brown; baste frequently with marinade.

Add lemon and orange slices to remaining marinade; heat and serve with chicken. Yield: 6 to 8 servings.

CHICKEN ORIENTAL

4 whole chicken breasts, halved
½ cup soy sauce
½ cup dry white wine
    Juice of 2 limes or 1 lemon
1 clove garlic, crushed
2 teaspoons curry powder
1 teaspoon ground ginger
1 teaspoon minced onion

Wash chicken and dry with paper towels. Combine all other ingredients for marinade. Put chicken in large, shallow glass or enameled dish; cover with marinade and refrigerate overnight, turning chicken several times. Drain and cook on grill about 15 minutes; turn and cook an additional 15 minutes or until chicken is done, basting often with sauce. Yield: 8 servings.

CHICKEN TERIYAKI

⅔ cup soy sauce
¼ cup white wine
2 tablespoons sugar
1 clove garlic, minced
1 tablespoon salad oil
½ teaspoon ground ginger
1 (2½-pound) fryer chicken, cut up

Combine soy sauce, wine, sugar, garlic, salad oil, and ginger. Marinate chicken in this mixture at least 1 hour or, preferably, overnight. Grill chicken for 30 minutes or until done, turning frequently and basting with marinade. Yield: 4 servings.

CHICK KABOBS

6 whole chicken breasts, boned
1 (2-ounce) can whole button mushrooms
1 (7½-ounce) can whole white onions
1 large green pepper, cut into 1-inch pieces
¼ cup salad oil
2 tablespoons vinegar
1 (8-ounce) can crushed pineapple, undrained
1 cup catsup
2 tablespoons soy sauce
1 teaspoon curry powder
¼ cup dried rosemary
2 tablespoons firmly packed brown sugar
1½ teaspoons salt
2 teaspoons pepper
1 tablespoon lemon juice
2 tablespoons cornstarch
1 cup water
2 cups cooked rice

Cut each chicken breast into 4 pieces, each about 1½ inches square. Alternate chicken, mushrooms, onions, and green pepper on 6 skewers. Combine salad oil, vinegar, pineapple, catsup, soy sauce, curry powder, rosemary, brown sugar, salt, pepper, and lemon juice. Pour over

skewers in shallow baking dish. Cover and refrigerate 4 to 6 hours before cooking. Grill 6 to 7 minutes over medium heat, basting with marinade occasionally. Turn, brush with marinade, and brown other side.

Combine cornstarch and water in saucepan; add remaining marinade and stir until smooth. Pour part of sauce over rice. Place skewers on rice; pour remaining sauce over kabobs. Yield: 6 servings.

POLLO ROLLEÑAS (CHICKEN ROLLS)

4 whole chicken breasts
1 small onion, chopped
2 cloves garlic, minced
2 tablespoons salad oil
3 fresh tomatoes, chopped
3 eggs, beaten
1 cup toasted almonds
1 teaspoon chopped parsley
Salt to taste
½ cup salad oil
Juice of 1 lemon
¼ cup water

Remove bones from chicken breasts, leaving each breast in one piece; set meat aside. Sauté onion and garlic in salad oil until lightly browned. Add tomatoes; stir in eggs and cook until eggs coagulate. Add almonds, parsley, and salt. Remove from heat and cool slightly. Stuff chicken breasts with this mixture; fasten with skewers. Broil over hot coals for 30 minutes or until chicken is tender, turning frequently. During the last 15 minutes of cooking time, brush chicken with basting sauce made by combining salad oil, lemon juice, and water. Yield: 4 servings.

CHICKEN IN THE POT

¼ cup butter
¼ cup salad oil
1 teaspoon salt
½ teaspoon pepper
2 cloves garlic, crushed
1 teaspoon monosodium glutamate
2 (1½- to 2-pound) frying-size
    chickens, cut into serving pieces
3 cups chicken broth
1 pound pearl onions
2 stalks celery and tops, coarsely
    chopped
5 large carrots, split lengthwise and
    halved
½ cup dry white wine
2 tablespoons all-purpose flour
⅓ cup water
1 pound fresh mushrooms, halved, or
    1 (8-ounce) can whole
    mushrooms, undrained
    Cooked wild rice

Combine butter, salad oil, salt, pepper, garlic, and monosodium glutamate in a large skillet; add chicken and cook until delicately browned. Transfer to Dutch oven; add chicken broth, onions, celery, and carrots. Simmer for 30 to 45 minutes or until chicken is tender. Add wine.

Combine flour and water; stir into chicken mixture. Add mushrooms; simmer 10 additional minutes, stirring frequently. Serve with wild rice. Yield: 6 to 8 servings.

CHICKEN À LA KING

½ cup chopped green pepper
⅔ cup butter or margarine
⅔ cup all-purpose flour
4 cups chicken broth
2 cups milk
2 teaspoons salt
1 teaspoon pepper
2 teaspoons paprika
1 egg yolk, slightly beaten
2 (4-ounce) cans pimientos, chopped
2 cups cooked, diced chicken
    Toasted bread crumbs

Sauté green pepper in butter; add flour and stir until smooth. Add chicken broth, milk, salt, pepper, and paprika. Cook slowly, stirring constantly, until slightly thickened. Add egg yolk gradually and stir for 1 minute. Add pimientos and chicken; simmer until all ingredients are heated thoroughly and mixture is thick. Top with toasted bread crumbs. Yield: 6 servings.

CHICKEN CACCIATORE

¼ cup olive oil
1 (2½- to 3-pound) broiler-fryer
    chicken, cut up
2 medium onions, cut in ¼-inch
    slices
2 cloves garlic, minced
1 (16-ounce) can tomatoes
1 (8-ounce) can seasoned tomato
    sauce
1 teaspoon salt
¼ teaspoon pepper
½ teaspoon celery seeds
1 or 2 bay leaves
1 teaspoon crushed oregano
    or basil
¼ cup California sauterne

Heat olive oil in skillet; add chicken pieces and brown slowly, turning once. Remove chicken from skillet; sauté onion and garlic in oil until tender, but not brown. Combine remaining ingredients, except wine. Return chicken to skillet; add sauce mixture. Cover and simmer 45 minutes. Stir in wine.

Cook uncovered, turning occasionally for 20 minutes or until fork tender. Remove bay leaves; skim off excess fat. Yield: 4 servings.

CHICKEN BREASTS RIVIERA

4 whole chicken breasts, boned
½ cup buttermilk
½ cup butter
¾ teaspoon salt
⅔ cup grated Parmesan cheese
1 tablespoon minced parsley
1 cup cooking sherry
1 (4-ounce) can sliced mushrooms, drained
   Parsley

Place chicken breasts in buttermilk while preparing fire. Line firebox of grill with aluminum foil. Allow coals to burn down until covered with a gray ash. Place butter in a skillet and place on grill. (Pan may be made by doubling foil and folding around sides to make a shallow edge.)

Remove chicken breasts from buttermilk and sprinkle with salt. Combine Parmesan cheese and parsley; coat both sides of chicken with this mixture. Place in skillet when butter is hot. After 5 minutes and when chicken breasts are well coated with butter, place the breasts on the open grill until they are a golden brown. Then place them back in skillet.

Pour sherry over chicken and simmer about 1 hour, basting frequently with sherry and butter from the pan. During the last 30 minutes, add mushrooms. Remove chicken to hot platter and spoon remaining sauce over it. Garnish with parsley. Yield: 4 servings.

CHICKEN À L'ORANGE

2½ tablespoons all-purpose flour
1 teaspoon chili powder
½ teaspoon salt
1 (2-pound) fryer, cut into pieces
3 tablespoons melted butter or margarine
1 tablespoon grated orange peel
1 cup orange juice
1 teaspoon sugar
1 orange, sectioned

Combine flour, chili powder, and salt; dredge chicken pieces, reserving remaining flour mixture. Brown chicken in melted butter over medium heat.

Remove chicken from skillet; stir in remaining flour mixture, orange peel, orange juice, and sugar. Return chicken to skillet; cover. Simmer 45 minutes or until chicken is tender. Remove cover; add orange sections, and heat 5 minutes. Yield: 2 or 3 servings.

MEDITERRANEAN CHICKEN WITH EGGPLANT

1 (2½- to 3-pound) broiler-fryer chicken, quartered
1½ teaspoons salt, divided
1 teaspoon Ac'cent
½ cup butter or margarine, divided
1 medium eggplant, cut into ½-inch slices (do not pare)
1 large onion, chopped
1 (16-ounce) can tomatoes
1 (8-ounce) can tomato sauce with mushrooms
¼ teaspoon ground dried basil
¼ teaspoon ground dried thyme
¼ teaspoon crushed dried oregano
¼ teaspoon hot sauce
   Hot buttered noodles
¼ cup grated Parmesan or Romano cheese

Sprinkle chicken with 1 teaspoon salt and Ac'cent. Heat 3 tablespoons butter in large skillet. Add chicken; brown on both sides; remove. Add 3 tablespoons butter to skillet; brown eggplant quickly on both sides over medium-high heat; remove. Add remaining 2 tablespoons butter to skillet; cook onion until tender but not brown; remove.

Layer eggplant slices and onion in skillet; top with chicken. Combine tomatoes, tomato sauce, remaining ½ teaspoon salt, herbs, and hot sauce. Pour over chicken. Cover and simmer 30 minutes or until chicken is tender. Serve over hot buttered noodles; sprinkle with cheese. Yield: 4 servings.

FAR EAST CHICKEN CHOW MEIN

1 cup chopped celery
½ cup chopped onion
1 green pepper, cut into strips
7 tablespoons melted butter or
    margarine, divided
¼ cup all-purpose flour
⅛ teaspoon curry powder
1 cup evaporated milk
3 tablespoons soy sauce
1 (17-ounce) can bean sprouts,
    undrained
2 tablespoons chopped pimiento
2 cups chopped cooked chicken
2 (5-ounce) cans Chinese noodles

Sauté celery, onion, and green pepper in 2 tablespoons butter; drain.

Combine 5 tablespoons butter, flour, and curry powder; blend until smooth and cook over low heat until bubbly.

Gradually add evaporated milk. Cook, stirring constantly, until smooth and thickened. Add soy sauce, bean sprouts, and pimiento to sauce, mixing well. Stir in sautéed vegetables and chicken. Serve hot over noodles. Yield: 6 to 8 servings.

DEEP SOUTH COUNTRY CAPTAIN

1 (3½-pound) young, tender hen
⅓ cup all-purpose flour
½ teaspoon salt
¼ teaspoon pepper
1¾ teaspoons Ac'cent
½ cup shortening
1 cup finely chopped onion
1½ cups finely chopped green
    pepper
1 clove garlic, finely chopped
1 teaspoon salt
½ teaspoon white pepper
2 teaspoons curry powder
2 (16-ounce) cans tomatoes
1 teaspoon chopped parsley
½ teaspoon ground dried thyme
2 cups hot cooked rice
¼ cup currants
1 cup toasted almonds
    Parsley for garnish (optional)

Cut chicken into frying-size pieces; remove skin. Combine flour, salt, pepper, and Ac'cent. Dredge chicken in flour mixture, coating evenly. Brown on all sides in hot shortening. Remove from skillet; put chicken in a warm place.

Add onion, green pepper, and garlic to drippings; cook very slowly, stirring constantly, until vegetables are tender. Add salt, pepper, curry powder, tomatoes, parsley, and thyme.

Put warm chicken pieces in roaster; pour tomato mixture over. If it does not cover the chicken, add a little water to the skillet and pour it out over the chicken. Cover and bake at 350° for 45 minutes or until tender.

To serve, put chicken in center of large heated platter; pile rice around it. Drop currants into hot sauce to plump them; pour over chicken. Scatter almonds over top. Garnish with parsley, if desired. Yield: 6 servings.

CHICKEN PAPRIKA

  Giblets
2 cups water
1 small onion
3 or 4 parsley sprigs
2 teaspoons salt, divided
4 peppercorns
1 bay leaf
¼ cup finely chopped onion
4 tablespoons butter, divided
1 cup all-purpose flour,
    divided
6 teaspoons paprika, divided
1 (2- to 3-pound) frying chicken,
    disjointed
⅓ cup half-and-half
⅓ cup strong coffee
1½ cups commercial sour cream

Place giblets in saucepan with 2 cups water, small onion, parsley, 1 teaspoon salt, peppercorns, and bay leaf. Cover; simmer 1 hour. Cook chopped onion in 2 tablespoons butter until soft, but not brown. Remove and set aside the onion, leaving butter in skillet. Combine flour (using all but 2 tablespoons), 1 teaspoon salt, and 2 teaspoons paprika in paper bag. Shake chicken pieces in bag until coated. Brown well in butter. Add 2 tablespoons giblet broth. Cook chicken, covered, slowly for 35 to 40 minutes or until tender.

Melt remaining 2 tablespoons butter in saucepan; blend in 2 tablespoons flour. Add 1 cup giblet broth, half-and-half, coffee, and 4 teaspoons paprika. Stir over low heat until smooth and thickened. Return onion to pan. Add sour cream gradually, stirring vigorously. Pour sauce over chicken in skillet; cook over low heat 3 minutes, turning chicken and stirring sauce. Do not boil. Yield: 4 servings.

CURRIED CHICKEN WITH RICE

5 tablespoons butter or margarine
½ cup minced onion
6 tablespoons all-purpose flour
2½ teaspoons curry powder
1¼ teaspoons salt
1½ teaspoons sugar
¼ teaspoon ground ginger
1 cup chicken bouillon
2 cups milk
1 teaspoon lemon juice
4 cups chopped cooked chicken
  Hot cooked rice

Melt butter over low heat; add onion and simmer until tender. Stir in flour, curry powder, salt, sugar, and ginger. Gradually stir in chicken bouillon (dissolve 1 chicken bouillon cube in 1 cup boiling water) and 2 cups milk. Cook over very low heat until mixture thickens, stirring occasionally. Add lemon juice and chopped chicken. Continue cooking until mixture is thoroughly heated. Serve with hot, cooked rice. Yield: 6 to 8 servings.

BRANDIED CHICKEN ANISE

1 clove garlic, minced
1 small onion, chopped
3 tablespoons melted butter
4 whole chicken breasts
  Salt to taste
1 chicken bouillon cube
½ cup water
½ cup brandy
¼ teaspoon anise seed

Sauté garlic and onion in butter in heavy skillet until transparent. Remove vegetables from skillet and brown chicken breasts in the butter. When chicken is brown on all sides, return garlic and onion to skillet. Add salt, bouillon cube, water, brandy, and anise seed.

Cover skillet and cook over low heat until chicken is tender, about 45 minutes. Yield: 4 servings.

COLD CHICKEN ITALIANO

2 (2½- to 3-pound) frying-size
  chickens, cut up
1½ cups salad oil
4 carrots, sliced
1 clove garlic, chopped
2 large onions, sliced
⅛ teaspoon ground dried thyme
⅛ teaspoon ground dried marjoram
2 bay leaves
12 peppercorns
1 teaspoon salt
3 cups vinegar
  Tomato wedges
  Stuffed olives

Sauté chicken in hot oil until brown. Remove from oil and put in a 3-quart casserole; add carrots, garlic, onion, spices, salt, and vinegar. Cover and simmer about 1½ hours or until chicken and vegetables are tender. Remove from heat, cool, and refrigerate. Serve cold; garnish with tomato wedges and stuffed olives. Yield: 8 servings.

CHICKEN LIVERS WITH SOUR CREAM

½ pound chicken livers
⅓ cup chopped onion
¼ cup chopped green pepper
2 tablespoons melted butter or
    margarine
2 hard-cooked eggs, diced
¾ cup commercial sour cream
½ teaspoon salt
    Dash pepper
¼ teaspoon Worcestershire sauce

Sauté chicken livers, onion, and green pepper in butter; add eggs and sour cream. Cook over low heat until cream is heated through (do not overcook because too much heat will cause mixture to curdle). Season with salt, pepper, and Worcestershire sauce. Yield: 2 servings.

LENTILS WITH CHICKEN CURRY

1 (16-ounce) package lentils
5 cups water
2 (2- to 3-pound) fryer chickens
1 carrot, diced
1 stalk celery, chopped
1 medium onion, cut in quarters
    Salt to taste
    Water
¾ cup minced onion
¼ cup butter
2 to 3 tablespoons curry powder
3 cups chicken broth, divided
4 egg yolks, beaten
1 cup half-and-half
    Condiments (optional)

Simmer lentils in 5 cups water for 45 minutes or until tender.

Combine chicken, carrot, celery, onion, and salt; cover with water and simmer until chicken is tender. Bone chicken and cut meat into bite-size pieces. Heat broth and strain; set broth and vegetables aside.

Sauté minced onion in butter until tender but not browned; add curry powder and cook a few minutes, stirring occasionally. Combine onion-curry mixture and 2 cups chicken broth in top of double boiler; simmer 10 minutes over hot water.

Let egg yolks and half-and-half come to room temperature; combine and beat well. Add about ¼ cup heated curry broth to egg yolk mixture; then stir mixture into the broth in double boiler; stir until thickened.

Combine reserved vegetables, chicken, and remaining chicken broth; heat thoroughly. Pour curry sauce over chicken mixture; ring with hot lentils. If desired, top with condiments (chopped peanuts, crisp crumbled bacon, white seedless raisins, flaked coconut, preserved kumquats, or chopped hard-cooked egg whites with sieved egg yolks). Yield: 8 servings.

CHICKEN À LA VALLÉE D'AUGE

4 to 5 whole broiler-fryer chicken
    breasts, boned
¼ cup butter or margarine
1 teaspoon salt
⅛ teaspoon pepper
6 shallots, minced, or 2 small onions
1 tablespoon chopped parsley
¼ teaspoon ground dried thyme
¼ teaspoon dried rosemary
¾ cup cider
½ cup half-and-half

Halve breasts. Brown chicken in butter in large skillet over low heat, about 20 minutes. Add remaining ingredients except half-and-half. Blend sauce well, cover, and simmer 15 minutes or until chicken is tender. Remove chicken breasts and keep warm. Add half-and-half to the pan liquid; stir and heat to serving temperature. Do not boil. Serve sauce over chicken or separately. Yield: 8 to 10 servings.

SHERRIED MUSHROOM CHICKEN

1 cup fresh mushrooms or 1
    (8-ounce) can, drained
4 tablespoons melted butter or
    margarine, divided
4 large whole chicken breasts,
    skinned and boned
1 teaspoon salt
¼ teaspoon pepper
⅛ teaspoon garlic salt (optional)
½ teaspoon paprika
¼ teaspoon crushed dried
    rosemary
¾ cup dry sherry
¼ cup water
1 teaspoon cornstarch
¼ cup minced green onions

Sauté mushrooms in 2 tablespoons butter; remove from pan and set aside. Wipe chicken dry with paper towel; brown chicken in 2 tablespoons butter. Sprinkle with salt, pepper, garlic salt, paprika, and rosemary. Add sherry. Cover pan; simmer about 30 to 40 minutes or until chicken is tender. Blend water and cornstarch and stir into the pan liquids. Add mushrooms and onions and cook for 30 minutes. Yield: 4 servings.

CHICKEN WATERZOIE

2 broiler-fryer chickens, cut in
    serving pieces
2 cups water
1 bay leaf
1 onion, stuck with 2 cloves
1 stalk celery
1½ teaspoons salt
⅛ teaspoon pepper
⅛ teaspoon ground dried thyme
¼ cup cold water
3 tablespoons all-purpose flour
2 egg yolks
2 tablespoons lemon juice
1 teaspoon sugar
    Parsley
    Lemon slices

Put chicken in pot with tight-fitting lid; add water, bay leaf, onion, celery, salt, pepper, and thyme; cover. Bring to a boil; reduce heat and simmer 40 minutes. Remove chicken. Strain broth and measure 2 cups into the pot. Stir water into flour to make a paste; add to broth in pot, stirring constantly. Bring to a boil. Beat egg yolks, lemon juice, and sugar with fork. Stir in a small amount of the hot mixture, then gradually add to broth, stirring constantly. Add chicken; heat. Turn into serving dish. Garnish with parsley and lemon slices. Yield: 8 to 10 servings.

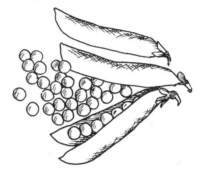

CHICKEN NEWBURG

1 small onion, chopped
3 tablespoons salad oil
3 tablespoons all-purpose flour
1 teaspoon salt
    Dash pepper
¼ teaspoon tarragon
1 cup chicken broth
½ cup milk
2 cups diced, cooked chicken
1 egg yolk, slightly beaten
1 tablespoon lemon juice
¼ cup sherry
1 pimiento, chopped
1 avocado, cubed
    Toasted bread

Cook onion in hot oil about 3 minutes. Stir in flour, seasonings, broth, and milk. Cook until mixture thickens, stirring constantly. Add chicken. Blend in egg yolk, lemon juice, sherry, pimiento, and avocado. Heat. Serve on toast. Yield: 4 to 6 servings.

SERBIAN CHICKEN PAPRIKAS

2 large onions, chopped
2 teaspoons salt
¼ cup salad oil
4 whole chicken breasts, boned and
    cut into chunks
½ cup water
1 tablespoon paprika
½ cup milk
2½ tablespoons all-purpose flour
    Cooked noodles
    Chopped fresh parsley (optional)

Sauté onion and salt in hot oil over medium heat until onions are tender and slightly golden. Add chicken, stirring occasionally until meat begins to brown. Add water and paprika; stir to remove any lumps. Cover; simmer about 30 minutes or until chicken is tender. Stir milk into flour until smooth; add to chicken and simmer 10 to 15 minutes. Serve over noodles and garnish with chopped parsley, if desired. Yield: 4 servings.

RIPE OLIVE PORTUGUESE CHICKEN

1 (3-pound) broiler-fryer chicken,
    quartered
¾ teaspoon salt
¼ teaspoon pepper
3 tablespoons melted butter or
    margarine
¼ cup chopped onion
1 clove garlic, minced
1 tablespoon all-purpose flour
1 (8-ounce) can tomatoes
¼ cup white wine or water
1 chicken bouillon cube
2 medium-size fresh tomatoes
1 cup ripe olives, pitted
1 tablespoon chopped parsley

Season chicken with salt and pepper. Brown chicken in butter in skillet. Remove chicken; add onion and garlic and cook until onion is transparent. Stir in flour. Add canned tomatoes, wine, and bouillon cube. Cook, stirring constantly, until sauce boils and thickens.

Return chicken pieces to pan; cover tightly and cook over very low heat for 30 to 35 minutes.

Core and cut fresh tomatoes into eighths. Add with olives to chicken mixture. Cover and cook 5 to 10 minutes longer. Place on serving dish, and sprinkle with parsley. Yield: 4 servings.

Note: In order to freeze, cool thoroughly just after the 30-minute cooking time. Seal and freeze. To serve, remove from freezer, thaw, add tomatoes and olives, and cook for 10 minutes.

SPANISH PAELLA

¾ cup olive oil
3 cloves garlic, minced
¼ pound lean pork, cut into chunks
3 whole chicken breasts, boned
    and cut into chunks
1 onion, chopped
1 green pepper, chopped
½ cup canned tomatoes
½ pound crawfish or Florida
    lobster, cut into chunks
½ pint oysters, drained
¼ pound scallops
½ pound shrimp, peeled and
    deveined
½ pound red snapper
2 quarts seafood broth
2½ cups rice
2 bay leaves
    Pinch saffron threads
    Dash yellow food coloring
1 tablespoon salt
    Small green peas, cooked
    Parsley
    Hard-cooked eggs, quartered
    Pimiento
    Cold, cooked asparagus
    White wine

Heat olive oil in a large casserole. Add garlic, pork, and chicken; cook until meat is tender. Add onion, green pepper, tomatoes, crawfish, oysters, scallops, shrimp, and red snapper (other seafood could be used). When seafood is almost done, add seafood broth and rice. Bring to a boil; then add bay leaves, saffron, food coloring, and salt. When rice begins to thicken, cover and bake at 350° for 15 minutes. Serve from casserole; garnish with green peas, parsley, eggs, pimiento, and asparagus. Sprinkle with white wine. Yield: 4 to 6 servings.

CHICKEN WITH PIMIENTO RICE

12 chicken thighs or 6 breasts, cut in
    half
    Salt and pepper
 3 tablespoons butter or margarine
 2 tablespoons sherry
⅓ cup minced onion
¼ cup all-purpose flour
1½ cups chicken broth
1½ cups commercial sour cream
 2 tomatoes, peeled and finely
    chopped
 1 bay leaf
 2 teaspoons salt
    Dash cayenne pepper
    Pimiento Rice

Season chicken pieces with salt and pepper. Brown in butter until golden on each side. Remove chicken from pan and set aside. Add sherry to pan. Add onion and cook until tender. Blend in flour and cook until golden brown. Stir in chicken broth and sour cream; blend until smooth. Add tomatoes, bay leaf, and seasonings. Arrange chicken pieces in sauce. Cover, reduce heat, and simmer 35 minutes or until tender. Serve over bed of Pimiento Rice. Yield: 6 servings.

Pimiento Rice:

 3 cups chicken broth
1½ cups uncooked regular rice
1½ tablespoons butter or
    margarine
1½ teaspoons salt
 3 tablespoons chopped
    parsley
 3 tablespoons diced pimiento

Combine broth, rice, butter and salt; heat to boiling. Stir once, cover, reduce heat, and simmer about 20 minutes or until rice is tender. Add parsley and pimiento. Toss lightly. Yield: 6 servings.

CHICKEN LIGURIAN

2 (2½-pound) frying chickens, cut
    into serving pieces
2 teaspoons salt
    Dash pepper
1 large onion, finely chopped
3 cloves garlic, minced
1 cup olive oil
½ teaspoon basil
½ teaspoon rosemary
2 or 3 bay leaves
2 cups sliced fresh mushrooms
1 cup dry white wine
2 tablespoons granulated chicken
    bouillon
1 cup boiling water
1 (7¾-ounce) can pitted green olives,
    drained

Wash and dry chicken; sprinkle with salt and pepper. Sauté onion and garlic in oil until yellow; add chicken.

When meat begins to brown, sprinkle with basil and rosemary; add bay leaves. Simmer for a few minutes; add mushrooms. Continue to simmer until chicken is almost dry; add wine.

Dissolve bouillon in water. When chicken is dry again, add bouillon and olives. Simmer until chicken is tender and liquid is almost absorbed. Yield: 8 servings.

CHICKEN THIGHS CONTINENTAL

6 chicken thighs
2 tablespoons melted butter or
    margarine
¾ cup mushrooms
1 (10¾-ounce) can condensed celery
    soup
2 cups water
2 tablespoons chopped parsley
¼ teaspoon salt
    Dash pepper
1 cup brown rice, uncooked

Brown chicken pieces in butter in a large skillet; add mushrooms and cook until lightly browned. Add soup, water, parsley, salt and pepper, and rice. Stir well. Cover skillet; simmer about 1 hour or until rice is done, stirring frequently the last few minutes of cooking. Yield: 4 to 6 servings.

SWEET-AND-SOUR CHICKEN LIVERS

1 (8-ounce) can pineapple chunks
1 (8¼-ounce) can seedless green
    grapes
1 pound chicken livers
5 tablespoons butter or margarine,
    divided
1 green pepper, cut into strips
1 green onion, diced
1 medium apple, peeled and diced
½ cup sliced mushrooms
3 tablespoons vinegar
1 tablespoon soy sauce
3 tablespoons water
3 tablespoons sugar
1 tablespoon cornstarch
1 teaspoon salt
    Hot cooked rice

Drain pineapple chunks and grapes, reserving juice from each; set aside.

Cook chicken livers in 3 tablespoons butter about 15 minutes or until done;

remove from skillet and set aside. Sauté pepper, onion, apple, mushrooms, pineapple, and grapes in 2 tablespoons butter in skillet.

Combine vinegar, soy sauce, and water; stir in sugar, cornstarch, and salt until mixed well. Add reserved juice.

Combine juice mixture with fruit-vegetable mixture; cook, stirring constantly, until smooth and slightly thick. Add chicken livers; heat thoroughly. Serve over rice. Yield: 6 to 8 servings.

CHICKEN AND DUMPLINGS

1 (5-pound) hen
    Boiling salted water
2 cups self-rising flour
¼ cup vegetable shortening
¾ cup boiling water
    Salt and pepper to taste

Cook hen in boiling salted water until tender; remove from broth. Cool chicken, cut from bone, and set aside. Measure 1 quart broth into large saucepan. Bring to a boil and add chicken.

Put flour in large bowl; cut in shortening with pastry blender or forks. Add boiling water, a small amount at a time. Shape mixture into a ball and roll to a thickness of ⅛ inch on a lightly floured board. Cut into strips. Drop strips into boiling broth, cover, and cook about 8 to 10 minutes. Add salt and pepper. Yield: 6 servings.

CAMPFIRE CHICKEN

2 pounds chicken pieces
2 tablespoons melted shortening
1 (11-ounce) can condensed tomato
    bisque soup
1 (3-ounce) can sliced mushrooms
    Dash pepper
1 (8-ounce) can cut green beans,
    drained
1 (8-ounce) can whole onions, drained

Brown chicken in shortening in skillet. Pour off drippings. Add soup, mushrooms, and pepper. Cover; cook over low heat for 45 minutes, stirring frequently. Add green beans and onions; cook 5 minutes lonter. Yield: 4 to 6 servings.

CHICKEN À LA VINSON

1 large broiler-fryer chicken
5 tablespoons all-purpose flour
Salt and pepper
Paprika
½ cup olive oil
2 medium-size onions, chopped
3 stalks celery, chopped
1 large clove garlic, minced
3 tablespoons chopped parsley
1 large green pepper, chopped
1 (4-ounce) can mushrooms
1 (6-ounce) jar marinated artichoke
    hearts
Italian seasoning
Wine to taste (optional)
Cooked long-grain or wild rice

Prepare chicken as for frying; disjoint and clean carefully. Place chicken in a paper bag in which the flour, salt, pepper, and paprika have been combined. Shake until chicken is coated with the mixture. Brown chicken in hot oil in heavy skillet. Remove from skillet and drain. Pour off part of the olive oil— leave just enough to cover bottom of skillet. Sauté onion, celery, garlic, parsley, and pepper in remaining oil.

Add juice from mushrooms and oil from artichokes to sautéed mixture. Return chicken to skillet. Simmer until chicken is tender. Add a small amount of Italian seasoning to the mixture. Add mushrooms, artichokes, and several tablespoons of wine, if desired, to the chicken just before serving.

Serve over long-grain rice or wild rice. Yield: 4 servings.

POULET MARENGO

6 large whole chicken breasts, split
    and skinned
½ cup melted margarine
1 teaspoon salt
¼ teaspoon Ac'cent
2 tablespoons chopped chives
1 tablespoon tomato paste
1½ cups chicken broth
1 (4-ounce) can sliced mushrooms,
    undrained
1 (16-ounce) package frozen lobster
    tails
3 ripe tomatoes, cut in wedges

Brown chicken breasts in margarine. Sprinkle with salt, Ac'cent, and chives; place, meat side down, in skillet. Combine tomato paste, chicken broth, and mushrooms and pour over chicken. Cover and let simmer until tender, about 45 minutes. Cook lobster according to package directions. Remove meat from shell and cut into bite-size pieces. About 5 minutes before serving, add lobster to chicken mixture. Remove to platter, using tomato wedges around edge as a garnish. Pour sauce from skillet over mixture. Yield: 6 servings.

CHICKEN LIVERS IN WINE SAUCE

1 pound chicken livers
    Ac'cent
½ cup all-purpose flour
½ teaspoon pepper
¾ teaspoon salt
¼ cup salad oil
½ cup dry white wine
1 tablespoon Worcestershire sauce

Wash livers; drain. Sprinkle with Ac'cent. Combine flour, pepper, and salt in a bag; place livers in bag, and shake until well coated. Sauté livers in oil until brown.

Combine wine and Worcestershire sauce; pour over livers. Cover tightly and simmer 30 minutes. Yield: 4 to 6 servings.

CHICKEN CREOLE

1 (2½- to 3-pound) broiler-fryer
    chicken, cut into serving pieces
1½ teaspoons salt, divided
½ teaspoon paprika
1 medium onion, sliced
1 medium green pepper, cut into
    strips
½ cup chopped celery
1 (16-ounce) can tomatoes
1 (3- or 4-ounce) can mushrooms
    (optional)
½ teaspoon dried leaf thyme

Sprinkle chicken pieces with ½ teaspoon
salt and paprika. Place under broiler
heat for 10 minutes or until browned,
turning once. Combine remaining
ingredients in large skillet. Bring to a
boil, cover and cook 10 minutes. Add
chicken. Cover; reduce heat and simmer
30 minutes or until tender. Yield: 4
servings.

CHICKEN KORMA

2 (3½-pound) frying-size chickens, cut
    into serving-size pieces
    Salt and pepper
1 cup buttermilk or yogurt
4 cloves garlic, minced and divided
¼ cup butter or margarine
2 onions, finely chopped
½ teaspoon ground ginger
2 whole cloves
2 teaspoons salt
2 teaspoons ground coriander
2 teaspoons ground almonds
¾ teaspoon ground turmeric
¾ teaspoon ground cumin seeds
¼ teaspoon ground pepper
¼ teaspoon ground chili peppers or
    cayenne

Sprinkle chicken pieces with salt and
pepper. Place in a large bowl; pour
buttermilk mixed with half the garlic
over chicken. Marinate at room
temperature for 2 hours or longer,
basting frequently.

Melt butter in a 3-quart casserole or
heavy saucepan or skillet. Add onion,
remaining garlic, ginger, cloves, and salt.
Sauté over low heat for 5 minutes,
stirring frequently.

Combine other ingredients and add to
sautéed mixture. Cook for 5 minutes,
stirring constantly. Add chicken and
marinade and stir well. Cover and cook
over low heat (or in 350° oven) for 1½ to
2 hours or until chicken is tender. Stir
occasionally. Yield: 4 servings.

CHICKEN AND ROLLED DUMPLINGS

1 (4- to 5-pound) hen
    Water
    Salt
    Rolled Dumplings

Disjoint chicken, barely cover with
water, and add salt. Simmer for 2 to 3
hours or until meat is tender. Add Rolled
Dumplings. Cover; boil gently for 8 to 10
minutes. Yield: 6 to 8 servings.

Rolled Dumplings:

2 cups all-purpose flour
2 teaspoons baking powder
1 teaspoon salt
⅓ cup shortening
½ cup milk

Combine flour, baking powder, and salt.
Cut in shortening. Add milk to make a
stiff dough. Roll out to about ⅛-inch
thickness, and cut into 1-inch squares, 1
to 1½-inch strips, or diamonds. Sprinkle
lightly with flour and drop into boiling
chicken stock.

CHICKEN JAMBALAYA

Salt and pepper
4 pounds of fryer chicken, cut into
  serving pieces
All-purpose flour
¼ cup salad oil
1 cup chopped onion
1 green pepper, chopped
4 stalks celery, chopped
1 cup chopped ham
1 (10-ounce) can whole tomatoes
6 cups chicken broth
2 cups uncooked regular rice
¼ cup chopped parsley
1 teaspoon ground dried thyme
1 or 2 cloves garlic, mashed
1 teaspoon Worcestershire sauce
Dash cayenne

Salt and pepper chicken and dredge with flour. Fry chicken in oil until golden brown. Remove and set aside on absorbent paper.

Sauté onion, pepper, and celery in oil until wilted; add ham, tomatoes, and broth. Simmer 30 minutes. Add rice, chicken pieces, parsley, thyme, garlic, Worcestershire sauce, and cayenne. Cook until rice has absorbed the liquid and is tender. Yield: 8 servings.

MAHARAJAH CHICKEN CURRY

½ cup chopped onion
1 clove garlic, minced
¼ cup salad oil
1 medium tomato, chopped
1 small bay leaf
½ teaspoon ground cinnamon
3 whole cloves
5 cups cubed uncooked chicken
1½ teaspoons salt
1 tablespoon curry powder
½ teaspoon ground dried cumin
½ teaspoon crushed dried coriander
Dash pepper
Pinch saffron threads
1½ cups water
¼ cup fresh coconut milk
Commercial saffron rice, cooked

Sauté onion and garlic in oil until tender, but not brown. Add tomato, bay leaf, cinnamon, and cloves; cover and cook 5 minutes. Add cubed chicken; simmer slowly, uncovered, about 30 minutes. Add salt, curry powder, cumin, coriander, pepper, saffron, and water. Cook slowly for 35 to 40 minutes or until chicken is tender. Blend in coconut milk. Serve over hot saffron rice. Yield: 6 to 8 servings.

Note: If you cannot obtain coconut milk, you can make a substitute by using the vacuum-packed, flaked coconut. To make ¼ cup of coconut milk, take ¼ cup flaked coconut and let it stand in ½ cup cold water until it is well soaked—about 20 minutes. Then squeeze the juice through muslin cloth. Repeat the process two or three times; each time the milk becomes richer and thicker.

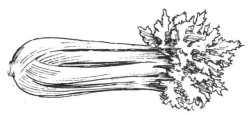

EXOTIC FRUITED CHICKEN CURRY

¼ cup butter or margarine
1 teaspoon finely chopped onion
¼ cup all-purpose flour
2 cups milk
1 teaspoon curry powder
1½ teaspoons salt
1½ cups diced cooked chicken
1 cup drained mandarin orange
  sections
1 cup seedless white grape halves
Hot cooked rice
½ cup toasted flaked coconut

Melt butter in blazer pan of chafing dish over direct heat; add onion and sauté. Blend in flour and gradually stir in milk. Cook, stirring constantly. Place over hot water. Add curry and salt and blend together. Add chicken and fruit and heat thoroughly. Serve over hot rice. Sprinkle with toasted coconut. Yield: 6 servings.

Cornish Game Hens

CORNISH GAME HENS WITH RICE STUFFING

6 Cornish game hens
¼ cup chopped onion
¼ cup butter or margarine
1⅓ cups packaged precooked rice
1 cup water
½ cup orange juice
2 teaspoons grated orange rind
2 tablespoons chopped parsley
1 cup chopped pecans
½ teaspoon sugar
¼ teaspoon poultry seasoning
1½ teaspoons salt
    Salt
    Melted butter or margarine

Rinse hens; pat dry. Sauté onion in butter until tender, but not browned. Add rice, water, orange juice, orange rind, parsley, pecans, and sugar. Mix just to moisten rice. Bring to a boil quickly over high heat. Cover, remove from heat, and let stand 5 minutes. Add poultry seasoning and salt; mix lightly with a fork.

Lightly salt inside cavity of each hen. Use approximately 1 cup of dressing for each hen, packing lightly. Place hens breast side up in uncovered pan; bake at 400° about 1 hour or until tender, basting frequently with melted butter. Yield: 6 servings.

HARVEST CORNISH HENS

3 Cornish game hens, halved
1½ teaspoons salt
1½ teaspoons monosodium glutamate
½ cup butter or margarine
1½ cups orange juice
2 tablespoons slivered orange peel
2 teaspoons instant minced onion
½ teaspoon ground ginger
¼ teaspoon hot pepper sauce
4 teaspoons cornstarch
    Water
½ cup toasted slivered almonds
2 oranges, sectioned
2 cups seedless grape clusters
    (optional)

Wash hens; pat dry. Sprinkle halves on both sides with salt and monosodium glutamate. Heat butter in large skillet. Add halves three at a time; brown on both sides, removing as browned. Return all halves to skillet; add orange juice and peel, onion, ginger, and hot pepper sauce. Simmer, covered, for 20 to 25 minutes or until tender. Arrange halves on heated platter; keep warm.

Blend cornstarch with a little cold water; stir into sauce in skillet. Cook, stirring constantly, until mixture thickens and comes to a boil. Add almonds, orange sections, and grapes, if desired. Heat gently. Pour a little sauce over hens. Serve remaining sauce separately. Yield: 6 servings.

TEXAS CORNISH GAME HENS

1 (15-ounce) can tamales
4 Cornish game hens
¼ cup honey
    Salt and pepper
1 teaspoon chili powder

Chop tamales. Wash hens and pat dry; use 2 chopped tamales to fill cavity of each hen. Combine honey, salt, pepper, and chili powder; rub outside of hen with honey mixture. Bake uncovered at 350° about 1 hour. Yield: 4 servings.

STUFFED CORNISH HENS

 6 Cornish game hens
½ lemon
 1 tablespoon salt
 2 teaspoons pepper
12 chicken livers
 5 tablespoons melted butter, divided
 6 medium mushrooms, sliced
½ cup chopped ham
¼ cup chopped toasted almonds
¼ cup melted butter
¼ cup dry white wine
 2 tablespoons red currant jelly

Wash hens and pat dry; rub cavities with lemon, salt, and pepper. Sauté chicken livers in 3 tablespoons butter; remove from heat and chop very finely. Sauté mushrooms in 2 tablespoons butter; combine livers, mushrooms, ham, and almonds to make dressing. Stuff hens lightly with dressing; skewer the openings and tie legs together. Combine ¼ cup butter, wine, and jelly; baste hens with this mixture. Place hens in shallow pan and put in smoker, or bake in oven at 350° for about an hour or until fork tender. Baste frequently. Yield: 6 servings.

CORNISH HEN-APPLE ROAST

 4 to 6 Cornish game hens
 1 teaspoon salt
½ teaspoon ground nutmeg
   Brown-Apple Stuffing (optional)
½ cup apple juice
 1 tablespoon lemon juice
½ cup butter, softened

Wash hens and pat dry. Rub inside and out with salt and nutmeg. Stuff lightly with Brown-Apple Stuffing (if dressing is desired) and truss. Combine apple juice and lemon juice. Set aside ¼ cup for basting and add remainder to softened butter. Spread mixture liberally over surface of birds. Roast at 350° for approximately 1 hour, brushing occasionally with basting liquid. Yield: 4 to 6 servings.

Brown-Apple Stuffing:

 4 Cornish game hen livers
 1 apple, peeled and sliced
 1 medium onion, peeled and sliced
¼ cup melted butter
 3 slices white bread
 3 slices whole wheat bread
½ teaspoon firmly packed brown sugar
 1 teaspoon salt
½ teaspoon pepper
½ teaspoon poultry seasoning

Sauté livers, apple, and onion in butter until lightly brown. Meanwhile, slightly moisten bread with water and break pieces quickly into bowl. Add brown sugar and seasonings to bread and mix lightly. Chop livers; add with onion and apple to bread mixture. Mix well; adjust seasonings to taste. Brown stuffing quickly in remaining butter in skillet, adding more if needed. Stuff lightly into cavities of birds. Yield: about 1½ cups.

CORNISH GAME HENS IMPERIAL

 3 Cornish game hens, halved
   Cooking sherry
 3 cups bread crumbs
1¼ cups grated Parmesan cheese
1½ cloves garlic, crushed
¼ teaspoon pepper
 3 teaspoons salt
 1 teaspoon parsley flakes
¾ cup chopped blanched almonds
¾ cup butter, melted and divided
   Butter
   Parsley

Rinse hens; pat dry. Marinate Cornish hens in cooking sherry to cover for 2 hours. Combine bread crumbs, Parmesan cheese, garlic, pepper, salt, parsley flakes, almonds, and ½ cup butter; mix well. Drain hens; dip each half in remaining butter; then roll in bread crumb mixture. Place halves in a 13- × 9- × 2-inch pan. Dot with butter. Bake at 350° about 1 hour. Garnish with parsley. Yield: 6 servings.

CORNISH GAME HENS CAPRI

4 Cornish game hens
1 teaspoon salt
1 teaspoon Italian herb seasoning
   mixture
4 sweet Italian (or other variety)
   sausages, halved
1 large green pepper, cut in eighths

Wash hens; pat dry. Split down middle; rub inside and out with salt and Italian seasoning mixture. Place hens, breast side down, on barbecue grill or oven broiler tray, and grill until brown, about 20 minutes. Grill sausages, turning to brown lightly on all sides. When hens are done on first side, turn and use poultry pins to skewer a section of green pepper topped with sausage on top of each Cornish hen. Prick sausages with fork so drippings add flavor during remainder of cooking period. Grill hens for approximately 20 minutes longer or until juicy, crisp, and well browned on underside. Yield: 4 servings.

ROASTED CORNISH HENS

2 Cornish game hens
   Rock salt
   Brown paper
   Salad oil

Wash hens; pat dry. Fill the bottom of an earthenware Dutch oven with rock salt. Place hens in Dutch oven and cover with brown paper which has been greased with salad oil. Bake at 300° about 1 hour or until done. Yield: 2 servings.

CORNISH GAME HENS WITH OYSTER DRESSING

4 Cornish game hens
1 pint oysters
2 small onions, chopped
2 tablespoons salad oil
4 tablespoons butter, divided
4 cups commercial packaged bread
   crumbs with herbs
   Salt and pepper

Wash hens; pat dry. Drain oysters; reserve liquid. Halve oysters. Sauté onion in oil; add oysters and cook until edges curl (about 10 minutes). Add 2 tablespoons butter and combine with bread crumbs. Add hot water to oyster liquid to make 1 cup; add to bread crumbs. Rub Cornish hens inside and outside with remaining butter and season with salt and pepper. Stuff hens; wrap individually in aluminum foil. Bake at 400° for approximately 1 hour. Fold back foil during last 10 or 15 minutes of cooking time, and let hens brown. Yield: 4 servings.

CORNISH GAME HENS À L'ORANGE

8 Cornish game hens
4 oranges, peeled and sliced
1½ cups orange juice
1½ teaspoons salt
¼ teaspoon pepper
½ cup firmly packed brown sugar
4 oranges, halved
4 teaspoons cranberry sauce
   Cooked wild rice

Rinse cavity and outside of hens; pat dry. Fill cavity of each hen with orange slices. Sew or skewer opening. Place hens, breast side up, in a roasting pan. Combine orange juice, salt, pepper, and brown sugar to make basting sauce. Roast hens uncovered at 450° for 15 minutes, brushing with basting mixture three times. Reduce oven temperature to 350° and roast 30 minutes longer, basting once or twice.

At end of baking time, remove skewers and orange stuffing (discard stuffing). Garnish with orange halves and a dollop of cranberry sauce in center of each. Serve with hot wild rice. Yield: 8 servings.

BATTER-FRIED CORNISH HENS

2 Cornish game hens
1 egg, beaten
¾ cup milk
1 cup all-purpose flour
1½ teaspoons salt
   Oil for frying

Wash, pat dry, and quarter Cornish game hens. Combine egg and milk; gradually add to flour mixed with salt; stir to a smooth batter. Dip hen in batter; deep fry in oil heated to 350°. Hens should be thoroughly cooked to a golden brown in approximately 15 minutes. Yield: 2 servings.

CORNISH HENS IN SWEET CIDER BASTING

4 to 6 Cornish game hens
   Brown-Apple Stuffing
¼ cup softened butter or
   margarine
1 teaspoon salt
¼ teaspoon ground nutmeg
¼ teaspoon ground sage
1 clove garlic, crushed
½ cup apple cider or apple juice
1 tablespoon lemon juice

Wash hens; pat dry. Stuff lightly with Brown-Apple Stuffing and truss. Place in roasting pan. Combine butter, salt, nutmeg, sage, and garlic; spread over hens. Combine apple cider and lemon juice; use as basting liquid. Pour half of liquid over birds. Roast at 350° for 1 hour or until drumstick moves easily in thigh joint, basting occasionally with reserved basting liquid and pan drippings. Yield: 4 to 6 servings.

Note: The recipe for Brown-Apple Stuffing is listed in this chapter under Cornish Hen-Apple Roast.

CORNISH GAME HENS CANTONESE

4 to 6 Cornish game hens
½ teaspoon ground ginger
¼ cup salad oil
½ cup orange juice
2 tablespoons honey
6 tablespoons chicken bouillon
1 tablespoon soy sauce
1 small clove garlic, crushed
1 large pineapple (quartered, peeled, and cored)

Wash hens; pat dry. Rub inside and out with ginger. Combine salad oil, orange juice, honey, bouillon, soy sauce, and garlic in bowl; pour mixture over birds and marinate 30 minutes to 1 hour. Alternate birds on skewer with pineapple cut into 2-inch wedges. Grill approximately 45 minutes, basting with marinade until juicy, crisp, and well browned. Yield: 4 to 6 servings.

CORNISH GAME HENS ORANGE

4 Cornish game hens
½ teaspoon pepper
1 teaspoon salt
½ teaspoon ginger
1 clove garlic, crushed
2 tablespoons lemon juice
4 tablespoons softened butter or
   margarine
4 small whole onions
4 carrots, sliced
¼ cup frozen orange juice
   concentrate
¼ cup giblet broth
1 teaspoon soy sauce

Wash hens; pat dry. Simmer giblets in salted water for broth. Combine seasonings, garlic, lemon juice, and butter; rub well into hens. Place hens in roasting pan. Surround with onions and carrots. Combine orange juice concentrate, broth, and soy sauce; use as basting liquid for hens. Roast at 350° about 1 hour. Yield: 4 servings.

Salads

JELLIED CHICKEN SALAD

2　envelopes (2 tablespoons)
　　unflavored gelatin
½　cup cold water
2　cups boiling water
1　teaspoon dillweed
1　teaspoon salt
1　tablespoon sugar
1　to 2 tablespoons wine vinegar
2　tablespoons lemon juice
1　tablespoon grated onion
6　to 8 thin cucumber slices
2　(4¾-ounce) cans chicken spread
1　cup finely chopped celery
2　tablespoons chopped pimiento
1　cup commercial sour cream
　　Salt and pepper to taste

Soften gelatin in cold water; dissolve in
boiling water. Combine half of gelatin
mixture with dill, salt, sugar, vinegar,
lemon juice, and onion; chill until
slightly thickened. Line edge of 1-quart
mold with cucumber slices; carefully pour
in the chilled gelatin. Chill until firm.
　Combine chicken spread, celery,
pimiento, and sour cream with remaining
gelatin mixture; season with salt and
pepper to taste. Chill until slightly
thickened; then spoon over firm gelatin
layer in mold. Refrigerate until firm.
Yield: 6 to 8 servings.

DIETER'S DINNER SALAD

1　head lettuce
1　teaspoon grated lemon rind
⅓　cup lemon juice
¼　cup corn oil
1　tablespoon honey
1　teaspoon salt
½　teaspoon celery seeds
¼　teaspoon garlic powder
3　dashes hot sauce
1　(16-ounce) can cut green beans
1　red apple
　　Lemon juice (optional)
2　cups cubed cooked chicken

Core, rinse, and thoroughly drain lettuce.
Refrigerate in plastic bag or plastic
crisper.
　To make dressing, combine lemon rind,
⅓ cup lemon juice, corn oil, honey, salt,
celery seeds, garlic powder, and hot
sauce; pour into a jar with a cover; chill.
　Just before serving, cut lettuce into
crosswise slices; then cut each slice
lengthwise and crosswise into bite-size
chunks; place on serving platter or in
individual salad bowls. Drain beans.
Quarter and core apple; slice thinly and
sprinkle with lemon juice, if desired.
Arrange beans, apple, and chicken on
lettuce. Serve with dressing. Yield: 6
servings.

CHICKEN SALAD SUPREME

2½　cups diced cooked chicken
1　cup finely chopped celery
1　cup seedless grapes
1　cup chopped walnuts or pecans
1　teaspoon minced onion
1　teaspoon salt
½　cup mayonnaise
½　cup whipped cream
　　Lettuce
　　Olives
　　Sweet pickles

Combine first 8 ingredients; chill. Serve
on lettuce, and garnish with olives and
pickles. Yield: 6 servings.

TOMATO STUFFED WITH CHICKEN

8 large tomatoes, cored
1¼ cups mayonnaise or salad dressing
1½ teaspoons curry powder
1 teaspoon salt
¼ teaspoon pepper
1½ teaspoons lemon juice
2 cups cooked rice
2 cups diced cooked chicken
1 cup diced celery
⅓ cup sliced green onion
1½ cups cooked peas
2 tablespoons diced pimiento

Scoop out tomato centers; turn upside down to drain. Chill.

Combine mayonnaise, curry powder, salt, pepper, and lemon juice. Add rice, chicken, celery, green onion, peas, and pimiento; mix well. Fill tomatoes with chicken mixture. Chill. Yield: 8 servings.

JELLIED CHICKEN ALMOND SALAD

1 envelope (1 tablespoon) unflavored gelatin
¼ cup cold water
1 cup mayonnaise
1 cup whipping cream, whipped
½ teaspoon salt
1½ cups diced cooked chicken
¾ cup chopped blanched almonds, toasted
¾ cup halved green seedless grapes
Lettuce
Sliced stuffed olives
Mayonnaise

Soften gelatin in cold water; dissolve over hot water. Cool slightly; then combine with mayonnaise, whipped cream, and salt. Fold in chicken, almonds, and grapes. Spoon into 6 or 8 individual salad molds. Chill until firm. Unmold on lettuce. Garnish with sliced stuffed olives and mayonnaise. Yield: 6 to 8 servings.

CHICKEN IN ASPIC

2 envelopes (2 tablespoons) unflavored gelatin
2 cups cold water, divided
2 (10½-ounce) cans condensed consommé
½ teaspoon salt
4 tablespoons lemon juice
2 cups diced cooked chicken
1 cup mixed cooked vegetables
½ cup chopped celery
4 tablespoons chopped green pepper
4 tablespoons chopped pimiento

Sprinkle gelatin on 1 cup cold water; let sit until gelatin has softened. Place over low heat and cook, stirring constantly, until gelatin is dissolved. Remove from heat; add remaining cold water, consommé, salt, and lemon juice. Chill until mixture is consistency of unbeaten egg white. Fold in remaining ingredients. Spoon into a 6-cup mold or individual molds. Chill until firm. Yield: 8 servings.

CONGEALED CHICKEN SALAD

2 envelopes (2 tablespoons) unflavored gelatin
½ cup cold water
1 cup mayonnaise
2 cups diced cooked chicken
1 teaspoon salt
½ cup diced celery
¼ cup chopped stuffed olives
3 tablespoons chopped pimiento
2 tablespoons finely chopped onion
3 tablespoons lemon juice
1½ teaspoons horseradish
2 tablespoons diced green pepper
¼ teaspoon paprika
1 cup chopped almonds
½ pint whipping cream, whipped

Soften gelatin in cold water; dissolve over hot water. Cool slightly and stir into mayonnaise. Add all other ingredients except whipped cream and mix well. Fold whipped cream into mixture. Put in oiled loafpan and chill until firm. Yield: 8 to 10 servings.

CELESTIAL CHICKEN SALAD

4 cups diced cooked chicken
2 cups diced celery
1 (4½-ounce) jar whole mushrooms, drained
½ cup pecan halves, toasted
4 slices bacon, fried and crumbled
1 cup mayonnaise or salad dressing
1 cup commercial sour cream
1½ teaspoons salt
2 tablespoons lemon juice
Lettuce (optional)

Combine chicken, celery, mushrooms, pecans, and bacon in a large bowl. Blend mayonnaise with remaining ingredients, except lettuce. Add to chicken mixture, tossing lightly to mix. Chill thoroughly. Serve in lettuce cups, if desired. Yield: 6 to 8 servings.

Note: Toast pecans in shallow baking pan at 350° about 15 minutes.

CHICKEN AND CARROT SALAD

2 cups diced cooked chicken
1 cup shredded carrot
¾ cup diced celery
½ cup slivered blanched almonds
2 tablespoons finely chopped onion
Salt to taste
1 tablespoon lemon juice
1 cup mayonnaise
Lettuce

Combine chicken, carrot, celery, almonds, onion, and salt. Combine lemon juice and mayonnaise; add to chicken mixture, and toss lightly. Chill. Serve on lettuce. Yield: 4 servings.

CHICKEN-AVOCADO SALAD

1 medium avocado
Juice of 1 lemon or lime, divided
1 teaspoon salt
1 (3¼-ounce) can pitted ripe olives, drained and quartered
2 cups chopped celery
2 cups chopped cooked chicken
½ cup mayonnaise
Lettuce
3 hard-cooked eggs, quartered
Pimiento strips

Peel avocado and cut into cubes; sprinkle with half of lemon juice and salt. Combine avocado, olives, celery, and chicken.

Combine mayonnaise and remaining lemon juice; add to chicken mixture, tossing gently to mix. Serve on lettuce, and garnish with eggs and pimiento. Yield: 6 servings.

CHICKEN AND FRUIT SALAD

2½ to 3 cups diced cooked chicken
1 cup sliced celery
2 tablespoons chopped green onion
2 tablespoons capers
1 teaspoon salt
2 tablespoons lemon juice
1 (8¼-ounce) can pineapple tidbits, drained
1 (11-ounce) can mandarin orange sections, drained
½ cup slivered almonds, toasted
½ cup mayonnaise
½ teaspoon grated lemon peel
Salad greens

Combine chicken, celery, green onion, capers, salt, and lemon juice. Cover and chill for several hours. Just before serving, add pineapple, orange sections (reserve a few for garnish), and almonds.

Combine mayonnaise and lemon peel; carefully fold into chicken mixture. Spoon into a bowl lined with salad greens. Garnish with reserved orange sections. Yield: 6 servings.

MOLDED CHICKEN SALAD

2 envelopes (2 tablespoons)
    unflavored gelatin
½ cup cold water
¾ cup mayonnaise or salad dressing
    Salt, pepper, paprika, and vinegar
    to taste
1 to 1½ cups diced cooked chicken
1 cup finely chopped celery
½ cup chopped olives
½ cup cooked, diced chestnuts
3 tablespoons chopped pimiento
    Several sprigs chopped parsley
    Carrot curls, radish roses, or other
    garnish

Soak gelatin in cold water; dissolve by
placing over hot water and stirring until
completely dissolved. Cool slightly, then
fold in mayonnaise, salt, pepper, paprika,
and vinegar to taste. Add other
ingredients and mix well. Spoon into an
oiled mold and refrigerate until
congealed. Unmold onto lettuce. Garnish
with carrot curls, radish roses, or other
colorful vegetables. Yield: 6 servings.

MOLDED CHICKEN LOAF

1 (4- to 5-pound) stewing chicken
2 teaspoons salt
3 or 4 peppercorns
1 carrot, sliced
1 onion, chopped
1 stalk celery, diced
2 envelopes (2 tablespoons)
    unflavored gelatin
2 cups cold water, divided
1 cup mayonnaise
1 cup half-and-half
¼ cup lemon juice
2 teaspoons Worcestershire sauce
1 tablespoon prepared horseradish
¼ cup chopped parsley
12 hard-cooked eggs, finely chopped
    Salad greens

Place chicken in large pan, and barely
cover with water; add salt, peppercorns,
carrot, onion, and celery. Cover; simmer

2½ to 3 hours or until chicken is tender.
Let chicken cool in broth; remove meat
from bones and cut into pieces.
  Soften gelatin in 1 cup cold water for 5
minutes, and dissolve over boiling water;
add remaining 1 cup cold water,
mayonnaise, half-and-half, lemon juice,
Worcestershire sauce, and horseradish;
blend well. Chill.
  When mixture begins to thicken, fold
in parsley, eggs, and chicken. Pour into 2
small loafpans. Chill until firm. Unmold
on crisp salad greens. Garnish as desired.
Yield: 16 servings.

CHICKEN LIVER SALAD

1 pound broiler-fryer
    chicken livers
1 teaspoon Ac'cent
1 teaspoon salt
1 teaspoon pepper
¼ cup corn oil
1 teaspoon crushed dried rosemary
½ cup chopped pimiento
1 tablespoon chopped onion
2 hard-cooked eggs, chopped
1 tablespoon chopped celery
    About ½ cup mayonnaise

Blot chicken livers dry. Sprinkle with
Ac'cent, salt, and pepper. Heat corn oil in
an 11-inch skillet over medium heat. Add
livers and cook slowly about 20 minutes.
Set aside; chop. Mix rosemary, pimiento,
onion, eggs, celery, and mayonnaise. (Use
more or less mayonnaise depending on
way served.) Mix and blend in chopped
liver. This mixture can be used as a dip,
sandwich filling, or salad served on
lettuce. Yield: 3 cups.

SUMMER BREEZE CHICKEN SALAD

2 (5-ounce) cans chicken, drained and diced
1 (5-ounce) can water chestnuts, drained and chopped
2 tablespoons chopped walnuts
¼ cup chopped green pepper
¼ teaspoon salt
⅓ cup commercial French dressing
    Sliced cucumbers
    Tomatoes, sliced ½ inch thick

Combine chicken, water chestnuts, walnuts, green pepper, salt, and French dressing; mix well. To serve, place a cucumber slice on a tomato slice and top with a scoop of chicken salad. Yield: 4 to 6 servings.

FAVORITE CHICKEN SALAD

½ cup salad dressing or mayonnaise
1 tablespoon lemon juice
1 (5- to 6-ounce) can boned chicken, diced
1 cup thinly sliced celery
2 tablespoons chopped pickles
1 small onion, chopped
    Salt and pepper to taste
    Lettuce

Combine salad dressing and lemon juice; add chicken, celery, pickles, and onion. Season with salt and pepper. Chill. Serve on crisp lettuce. Yield: 4 servings.

HOT CHICKEN SALAD DELUXE

½ cup sliced almonds
1 tablespoon melted margarine
2 cups diced cooked chicken
1 cup diced celery
½ teaspoon salt
½ teaspoon Ac'cent
2 teaspoons grated onion
½ cup mayonnaise
½ cup condensed cream of mushroom soup
½ cup shredded Cheddar cheese
½ cup crushed potato chips

Sauté almonds in margarine; drain. Combine all ingredients except potato chips. Spoon into a lightly greased 1-quart casserole; sprinkle with potato chips. Bake at 425° for 20 minutes. Yield: 4 to 6 servings.

CHICKEN SALAD WITH AVOCADO

3 cups diced cooked chicken
½ cup diced celery
1 cup sliced pitted black olives
⅓ cup mayonnaise
1½ cups diced avocado (½-inch pieces)
1 tablespoon lemon juice
    Dash cayenne pepper
    Lettuce
    Sliced olives or avocado (optional)

Combine chicken, celery, olives, and mayonnaise. Cut avocado just before serving and sprinkle with lemon juice. Fold avocado into chicken mixture and season with cayenne. Serve in lettuce cups and garnish, if desired, with olive or avocado slices. Yield: 6 servings.

DELUXE CURRIED CHICKEN SALAD

1½ cups cooked rice
2 tablespoons salad oil
1 tablespoon vinegar
1 teaspoon salt
¾ teaspoon curry powder
2 cups cubed cooked chicken
1 cup chopped celery
¼ cup chopped green pepper
1 (10-ounce) package frozen peas, cooked and drained
¾ cup mayonnaise
    Lettuce

Combine rice, salad oil, vinegar, salt, and curry powder; chill overnight. Combine chicken, celery, green pepper, peas, and mayonnaise; combine with rice mixture and chill several hours. Serve on lettuce. Yield: 8 servings.

CURRIED CHICKEN SALAD

1¼ cups mayonnaise or salad
    dressing
1½ teaspoons curry powder
 1 teaspoon salt
 ¼ teaspoon pepper
1½ tablespoons lemon juice
 2 cups cooked rice
 2 cups cooked diced chicken
 1 cup diced celery
 ⅓ cup sliced green onions
1½ cups cooked peas
 2 tablespoons diced pimiento

Combine mayonnaise, curry powder, salt,
pepper, and lemon juice; stir well. Add
rice, chicken, celery, green onions, peas,
and pimiento; mix well. Chill about 2
hours. Yield: 6 servings.

CHICKEN AND
PINEAPPLE SALAD

1 (8¼-ounce) can crushed
    pineapple
1 envelope (1 tablespoon)
    unflavored gelatin
1½ cups chicken stock, divided
 ½ teaspoon salt
 2 tablespoons lemon juice
1½ cups diced cooked chicken
 ½ cup diced celery
    Salad greens

Drain pineapple; reserve ¼ cup juice.
Sprinkle gelatin on ½ cup chicken stock
to soften; place over low heat and stir
until gelatin is dissolved. Remove from
heat and stir in remaining chicken stock,
salt, lemon juice, and reserved pineapple
juice. Chill to consistency of egg white.
    Fold in chicken, pineapple, and celery.
Turn into a 4-cup mold and chill until
firm. Unmold; garnish with salad greens.
Yield: 4 to 6 servings.

CHICKEN SALAD

1 envelope (1 tablespoon) unflavored
    gelatin
¼ cup cold water
1 cup mayonnaise
1 cup whipping cream, whipped
½ teaspoon salt
2 cups diced cooked chicken
¾ cup blanched, toasted, and
    chopped almonds
¾ cup seedless green grapes

Soak gelatin in cold water; dissolve over
hot water. Cool mixture; add
mayonnaise, whipped cream, and salt.
Fold in remaining ingredients; chill until
firm. Yield: 8 servings.

SALMAGUNDI

 3 quarts salad greens (Boston,
    romaine, endive, and watercress)
 1 pound cooked ham, cut into
    julienne strips
 1 pound chicken or turkey, cut into
    julienne strips
 4 hard-cooked eggs, sliced
16 sweet gherkins
 8 celery hearts
16 sardines
16 anchovy filets
    Oil and Vinegar Dressing

Arrange salad greens on individual salad
plates or on a large platter. Place ham,
chicken, eggs, gherkins, celery, sardines,
and anchovies in a pattern over and
around the salad greens. Sprinkle lightly
with Oil and Vinegar Dressing. Yield: 8
servings.

Oil and Vinegar Dressing:

1 teaspoon salt
¾ teaspoon white pepper
½ cup cider vinegar
½ cup salad oil

Combine all ingredients in a jar; cover
tightly. Shake well to blend before
serving. Yield: 1 cup.

CHICKEN-APRICOT SALAD

½ cup mayonnaise
1 cup commercial sour cream
¼ cup milk
2 tablespoons lemon juice
2 teaspoons prepared mustard
1 teaspoon salt
1 cup dried apricots, diced
3 cups diced cooked chicken
1 cup chopped celery
⅓ cup finely chopped scallions
Lettuce

Blend mayonnaise, sour cream, milk, lemon juice, mustard, and salt in large bowl; add apricots, chicken, celery, and scallions. Toss lightly until combined; chill. Spoon salad into lettuce-lined bowl. Yield: 6 servings.

HOT CHICKEN SALAD

2 cups diced cooked chicken
1 cup thinly sliced celery
½ cup cashews
½ teaspoon salt
1 onion, grated
1 cup mayonnaise
2 tablespoons lemon juice
½ cup shredded sharp Cheddar
    cheese
1 cup crushed potato chips

Combine all ingredients except cheese and potato chips. Pile lightly in casserole or individual baking dishes. Sprinkle with cheese and potato chips. Bake at 400° about 20 minutes or until mixture is heated and cheese is melted. Yield: 6 servings.

CHICKEN RAMBLER SALAD

Salad greens, torn into bite-size
    pieces
1 medium onion, chopped
1 (16-ounce) can or jar sliced pickled
    beets, drained
1 (16-ounce) can peas, drained
1 (5-ounce) can boned chicken or
    turkey, cut into bite-size pieces
2 hard-cooked eggs, sliced
Commercial French dressing or
    mayonnaise

Combine salad greens and onion and place in serving dish. Arrange beets, peas, chicken, and eggs on the greens. Serve with French dressing. Yield: 6 servings.

CHICKEN-RICE SALAD

1 tablespoon lemon juice
¾ cup mayonnaise or
    salad dressing
½ cup sliced stuffed green olives
2 cups cooked rice
2 cups diced cooked chicken
1 cup diced celery
2 tablespoons thinly sliced green
    onion
¼ cup sliced almonds, toasted
6 lettuce cups

Combine lemon juice and mayonnaise; blend well. Combine with remaining ingredients except lettuce cups; mix lightly and chill. Serve in individual lettuce cups; garnish with additional sliced olives. Yield: 6 servings.

Sandwiches

CHICKEN SPREAD

¼ cup mayonnaise
1 (5-ounce) can boned chicken, chopped
¼ green pepper, cut in strips
1 stalk celery, sliced
1 pimiento
½ teaspoon salt

Place all ingredients in blender. Cover; blend at high speed for 20 seconds. Yield: 1¼ cups (2 to 3 servings).

CHICKEN AND MUSHROOM SANDWICH SPREAD

1 cup chopped cooked chicken
⅓ cup toasted almonds (optional)
1 tablespoon minced onion
1 (3-ounce) can broiled mushrooms, chopped
½ cup diced celery
½ teaspoon salt
⅛ teaspoon pepper
½ teaspoon curry powder
½ cup mayonnaise

Put chopped chicken (preferably white meat) through food chopper, using fine cutter. Measure 1 cup and set aside. Put almonds through food chopper. Combine chicken with other ingredients; mix well. Yield: 1½ to 2 cups (3 to 4 servings).

BROILED CHICKENBURGERS

12 round buns
   Butter or margarine
1 (16-ounce) can jellied cranberry sauce, cut into 12 slices
3 cups chopped cooked chicken
⅔ cup mayonnaise or salad dressing
½ cup pickle relish
¾ teaspoon salt
   Dash pepper

Split buns and spread with butter. Place slice of cranberry sauce on bottom half of each bun. Combine chicken, mayonnaise, pickle relish, salt, and pepper; spread on top of cranberry sauce. Place under broiler until mixture is hot and bubbly, about 2 to 3 minutes. Cover with bun tops. Yield: 12 sandwiches.

CHICKEN GO-ROUNDS

4 slices white toast
12 to 16 tomato slices
1 (4¾-ounce) can chicken spread
2 tablespoons chopped fresh chives
¾ cup cottage cheese

Cover each toast slice with 3 to 4 tomato slices. Combine chicken spread and chopped chives; spoon onto center of toast. Surround chicken spread mixture with a ring of cottage cheese. Yield: 4 open-face sandwiches.

CURRIED CHICKEN SANDWICHES

3 cups diced cooked chicken
½ cup diced celery
½ cup diced unpeeled apple
⅓ cup mayonnaise
½ teaspoon salt
1 teaspoon curry powder
1 tablespoon lemon juice
   White pepper to taste
16 slices buttered bread

Combine first 8 ingredients and mix well. Spread on 8 slices of the buttered bread; top with remaining slices. Yield: 8 sandwiches.

71

HOT CHICKEN SANDWICHES

3 tablespoons melted butter
3 tablespoons all-purpose flour
½ teaspoon salt
½ teaspoon prepared mustard
2 cups milk
1½ cups shredded pasteurized
    process American cheese
    Cooked chicken, sliced or diced
    Toast
    Paprika
    Tomato slices
    Cooked bacon
    Chopped green chiles (optional)

Combine butter, flour, salt, and mustard
in top of double boiler; cook over medium
heat until bubbly. Add milk; stir until
sauce is smooth and thickened. Add
cheese and cook until melted. Place
chicken on toast and pour sauce over.
Sprinkle with paprika. Bake at 450° for
10 minutes. Serve with tomato slices and
bacon. If desired, garnish with chopped
green chiles. Yield: 2½ cups sauce (about
6 servings).

HOT BROWN SANDWICHES

2 tablespoons all-purpose flour
2 tablespoons melted margarine
1 teaspoon salt
⅛ teaspoon white pepper
1 cup milk
¼ to ½ cup shredded Cheddar cheese
    Sliced chicken
4 slices bread, toasted
8 slices bacon, cooked
¼ cup grated Parmesan cheese

Combine flour and margarine; cook over
low heat, blending until smooth. Stir in
salt and pepper. Gradually add milk,
stirring constantly, until smooth and
thickened. Add Cheddar cheese, stirring
until melted.
    Place chicken on toast, and cover with
sauce. Place 2 slices bacon on each
sandwich, and sprinkle with Parmesan
cheese. Bake at 400° for 10 minutes or
until Parmesan melts. Yield: 4 servings.

BAKED CHICKEN SANDWICHES

1½ cups chopped cooked chicken
1 (10¾-ounce) can cream of
    mushroom soup
1 (10½-ounce) can chicken gravy
2 tablespoons chopped pimiento
2 tablespoons chopped onion
1 cup sliced water chestnuts
20 slices bread
4 eggs, beaten
2 tablespoons milk
    Crushed potato chips

Combine chicken, mushroom soup, gravy,
pimiento, onion, and water chestnuts.
Cut crusts from bread. Spread mixture
on bread and cover with a slice of bread.
Wrap individual sandwiches in plastic
wrap and freeze.
    Dip sandwiches, still frozen, in mixture
of beaten eggs and milk. Coat with
crushed potato chips and place on cookie
sheet. Bake at 300° for 1 hour. Yield: 10
sandwiches.

CHICKEN SPREAD MOSAICS

10 thin slices white bread
10 thin slices whole wheat bread
    Jellied cranberry sauce
1 (4¾-ounce) can chicken spread

Cut a 2½-inch scalloped round from each
slice of bread. With a 1¼-inch round
cutter, remove centers from 5 white and
5 whole wheat scalloped rounds. Replace
whole wheat centers with white centers
and white centers with whole wheat
centers. Spread remaining 10 rounds
with cranberry sauce, then with chicken
spread. Close sandwiches. Yield: 10
sandwiches.

Sauces, Gravies, and Marinades

TANGY BARBECUE SAUCE

1 cup catsup
½ to 1 teaspoon hot sauce
2 tablespoons firmly packed light
    brown sugar
1 teaspoon dry mustard
2 tablespoons wine vinegar
½ teaspoon ground dried thyme
¼ cup salad oil

Combine all ingredients and heat just to boiling before using to brush on chicken as it barbecues on grill. Yield: enough sauce for 1 (2½-pound) chicken, cut into serving pieces or halves.

EASY BARBECUE SAUCE

1 (8-ounce) can tomato sauce
⅓ cup catsup
1½ teaspoons vinegar
    Dash salt and pepper
½ teaspoon Italian seasoning
1 teaspoon prepared mustard
2 teaspoons commercial French
    dressing
2 teaspoons firmly packed brown
    sugar
1 tablespoon butter or margarine
¼ cup chopped onion

Combine all ingredients, mixing well. Simmer 15 to 20 minutes. Baste on chicken while grilling. Yield: 1⅓ cups.

MILD BARBECUE SAUCE

½ cup finely chopped onions
¼ cup melted margarine
1⅓ cups water
⅔ cup catsup
⅔ cup tomato juice
1½ teaspoons salt
1½ teaspoons paprika
1 teaspoon pepper
1 teaspoon Worcestershire sauce
½ teaspoon garlic salt

Sauté onion in margarine. Add other ingredients and bring to a boil. Use as a mopping sauce for barbecuing chicken. Yield: 3 cups, or enough sauce for 6 chickens.

UNBEATABLE BARBECUE SAUCE

1 (12-ounce) can beer
    Juice of 1 lemon
1 clove garlic, pressed
1 medium onion, chopped
¼ cup sugar
⅓ cup Worcestershire sauce
⅔ cup catsup
⅓ cup orange juice

Combine all ingredients and cook over medium heat until mixture comes to a boil. Lower heat and simmer for 15 minutes. Brush sauce on chicken while grilling. Yield: 3 cups.

SUPER BARBECUE SAUCE

½ cup red wine
½ cup salad oil
2 tablespoons grated onion
1 clove garlic, crushed
1 tablespoon salt
½ teaspoon pepper
2 teaspoons Worcestershire sauce
¼ teaspoon ground dried thyme
2 tablespoons lemon juice

Combine all ingredients, but do not heat. Use to brush on chicken as it cooks on grill. Yield: 1¼ cups.

BARBECUE SAUCE FOR CHICKEN

1 small onion, finely chopped
2 tablespoons bacon drippings
1 tablespoon Worcestershire sauce
⅔ cup tomato catsup
1 tablespoon vinegar
3 tablespoons lemon juice
2 tablespoons prepared mustard
1 cup chicken broth

Sauté onion in bacon drippings until soft and light yellow. Add remaining ingredients and simmer slowly 15 minutes or until fairly thick. Serve as sauce with grilled chicken. Yield: about 2 cups.

ONION BARBECUE SAUCE

1 (10¾-ounce) can condensed cream
   of mushroom soup
1 (10¾-ounce) can condensed onion
   soup
½ cup catsup
¼ cup salad oil
¼ cup vinegar
2 cloves garlic, minced
2 tablespoons firmly packed brown
   sugar
1 tablespoon Worcestershire sauce
⅛ teaspoon hot sauce

Combine all ingredients. Cover and cook over low heat about 15 minutes, stirring occasionally. Use to baste chicken while grilling. Yield: 2½ cups.

SOUTHERN BARBECUE SAUCE

1 cup water
2 cups vinegar
2 teaspoons pepper
1 cup melted margarine
2 tablespoons salt
   Garlic salt

Combine all ingredients in heavy saucepan; heat and place container on grill to use as a mopping sauce for chickens. Yield: about 4 cups.

SUPER-DUPER BARBECUE SAUCE

1 cup catsup
1 cup water
1 small onion, chopped
1 tablespoon Worcestershire sauce
¼ cup vinegar
1 tablespoon firmly packed brown
   sugar
2 teaspoons dry mustard
1 teaspoon paprika
1 teaspoon chili powder
1 clove garlic, minced
½ teaspoon meat tenderizer

Combine ingredients; cover and simmer slowly for 30 minutes. Sauce may be used to marinate chicken before grilling or to baste chicken during cooking. Yield: about 2 cups.

SWEET-AND-SOUR BARBECUE SAUCE

2 cups catsup
½ cup vinegar
½ cup water
1 cup sugar
½ cup firmly packed brown sugar
2 teaspoons onion salt
1 teaspoon celery salt
½ teaspoon ground cinnamon
½ teaspoon ground cloves
½ teaspoon ground allspice

Combine all ingredients, mixing well. Simmer over low heat for 1 hour. Use to baste chicken while grilling. Yield: 3 cups.

CHILI-PINEAPPLE SAUCE

1 (14-ounce) bottle catsup
1 cup pineapple juice
¾ cup chopped green onions
½ teaspoon chili powder

Combine all ingredients; stir until well blended. Baste poultry with sauce during grilling. Serve additional sauce with meat. Yield: 1½ cups.

BANG-UP BARBECUE SAUCE

1 (10¾-ounce) can condensed tomato
    soup
¼ cup sweet pickle relish
¼ cup chopped onion
1 tablespoon firmly packed brown
    sugar
1 tablespoon vinegar
1 tablespoon Worcestershire sauce

Combine all ingredients in saucepan;
cover and simmer until onion is tender
and flavors are blended. Baste chicken
while grilling. Yield: 1¾ cups.

BARBECUE SAUCE WITH A DIFFERENCE

½ cup salad oil
1 cup lemon juice
1 tablespoon salt
2 tablespoons molasses
1 teaspoon hot sauce

Combine salad oil, lemon juice, salt,
molasses, and hot sauce in a heavy
saucepan. Heat to boiling and use to
baste chickens on grill. Yield: about 1½
cups.

CREAM GRAVY FOR FRIED CHICKEN

3 tablespoons oil (reserved from oil
    used to fry chicken)
3 tablespoons all-purpose flour
    Salt and pepper to taste
1½ cups milk

Pour off all except 3 tablespoons of oil in
which chicken was fried. Turn heat to
high, add 3 tablespoons all-purpose flour,
and stir, scraping the browned bits from
bottom and sides of skillet. Flour may be
browned or stirred just until well mixed
with oil. Add salt and pepper; then add
1½ cups milk, stirring constantly as milk
is added. Cook until gravy is medium
thick. Add more salt and pepper, if
needed, and serve hot. Yield: about 1 cup.

BROWN POULTRY GRAVY

¼ cup all-purpose flour
2 to 4 tablespoons poultry fat from
    drippings
2 cups poultry broth, milk, or water
    Salt and pepper to taste

Blend flour into drippings. Brown over
low heat. (If brown drippings are used, it
is not necessary to brown the flour.)
    Add liquid slowly while stirring
constantly.
    Cook until gravy thickens, stirring
constantly. Season. Yield: 2 cups.
    Note: Add ½ cup chopped, cooked
giblets for giblet gravy.

WINE MARINADE

¼ cup salad oil
½ cup white wine
1 clove garlic, grated
1 small onion, grated
½ teaspoon salt
½ teaspoon celery salt
½ teaspoon pepper
¼ teaspoon crushed dried thyme
    leaves
¼ teaspoon crushed dried marjoram
    leaves
¼ teaspoon dried rosemary

Combine all ingredients and chill for
several hours. Marinate chicken in sauce
in refrigerator for 3 hours. Brush
marinade on chicken when grilling.
Yield: ¾ cup.

OIL AND VINEGAR MARINADE

½ cup salad oil
⅓ cup wine vinegar
1 clove garlic, minced
½ teaspoon salt
¼ teaspoon pepper

Combine all ingredients in a jar; cover.
Shake well and chill. Shake well before
pouring over chicken for marinating.
Yield: ¾ cup.

Soups and Stews

CURRIED CHICKEN NOODLE SOUP

1 medium-size green pepper,
    chopped
½ medium onion, finely diced
½ cup diced celery
2 cloves garlic,
    finely chopped
3 tablespoons melted butter or
    margarine
2 quarts chicken broth
½ teaspoon curry powder
⅛ teaspoon hot sauce
½ teaspoon Worcestershire sauce
    Salt and pepper to taste
1 cup uncooked narrow
    egg noodles
    Boiling salted water
1 cup diced cooked chicken
1 (8¼-ounce) can pineapple tidbits,
    drained
2 tablespoons chopped pimiento
¼ cup sherry

Sauté green pepper, onion, celery, and garlic in melted butter just until tender. Add chicken broth and seasonings; simmer about 10 minutes.

Cook noodles in boiling salted water until tender; drain and add to broth mixture. Add chicken, pineapple, pimiento, and sherry; simmer 10 minutes longer. Yield: 10 servings.

CHICK-A-VEG SOUP

1 (10¾-ounce) can condensed cream
    of chicken soup
1 (10¾-ounce) can condensed chicken
    gumbo soup
2 soup cans water
    Bacon bits, watercress, cheese
    crackers, or diced ham

Combine soups and water in a large saucepan; heat, stirring occasionally. Garnish with crisp bacon bits, chopped watercress, cheese crackers, or diced ham. Yield: 4 to 6 servings.

CURRIED CHICKEN SOUP

½ cup diced celery
¼ cup minced onion
¼ cup melted butter
¼ cup all-purpose flour
1 teaspoon salt
⅛ teaspoon pepper
1 to 1½ teaspoons curry powder
1 quart milk
2 cups diced cooked chicken
¼ cup chopped parsley

Sauté celery and onion in butter over low heat until tender. Blend in flour and seasonings. Add milk, and cook, stirring constantly, until smooth and thickened. Add chicken and heat thoroughly. Add parsley just before serving. Serve in hot bowls. Yield: 6 servings.

CHICKEN NOODLE-CRESS SOUP

1 quart seasoned chicken broth
½ cup finely diced carrots
¼ bunch watercress
½ cup finely diced cooked chicken
1 cup cooked fine egg noodles

Heat chicken broth; add carrots, watercress stems cut in ⅛-inch lengths, and chicken. Cook 10 minutes. Add noodles and coarsely cut watercress leaves. Heat thoroughly and serve immediately. Yield: about 4 servings.

CHICKEN BROTH

4 pounds chicken pieces
1 onion, quartered
2 stalks celery
½ teaspoon parsley flakes
1 bay leaf
¼ teaspoon ground dried thyme
⅛ teaspoon ground dried marjoram
2 quarts water
    Salt and pepper to taste

Combine chicken and remaining ingredients in a large kettle. Cover and bring to a boil; reduce heat and simmer 3 hours or until meat falls from bones. Strain broth; reserve chicken and vegetables for other uses. Cool and skim off fat. Cover and refrigerate until ready to use. Yield: about 1½ quarts.
    Note: Canned chicken broth, chicken broth made with bouillon cubes, or chicken concentrate may be substituted for freshly made chicken broth.

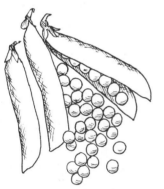

CLAM AND CHICKEN SOUP

2 (10¾-ounce) cans condensed cream
    of chicken soup
2 (10¾-ounce) cans condensed beef
    consommé
2 medium onions, chopped
2 (4-ounce) cans minced clams,
    drained and juice reserved

Combine soup, consommé, onion, and clam juice in top of double boiler. Simmer for 20 minutes. Add clams last, and cook just long enough to heat through. Yield: 8 servings.

OLIVE CREAM OF CHICKEN SOUP

2 quarts chicken broth
½ teaspoon ground dried thyme
½ cup chopped onion
1 cup grated carrots
2 cups diced cooked chicken
⅓ cup all-purpose flour
1½ cups milk
½ cup sliced pimiento-stuffed green
    olives
2 tablespoons chopped parsley
    Salt and pepper to taste

Heat chicken broth to boiling. Add thyme, onion, carrot, and chicken. Cover and cook until onion is tender. Combine flour and milk; mix until smooth and add to chicken mixture. Cook over low heat until thickened, stirring constantly. Add olives, parsley, salt, and pepper. Yield: about 10 servings.

CHICKEN CHOWDER

1 (2-pound) frying chicken
2½ cups water
1 small onion, peeled and sliced
1 cup chopped celery tops
1½ teaspoons salt
8 peppercorns
1 bay leaf
    Water
½ cup finely chopped onion
1 teaspoon curry powder
2 tablespoons butter or margarine
1 cup half-and-half
1 (16-ounce) can cream-style corn

Simmer chicken with water, sliced onion, celery tops, salt, peppercorns, and bay leaf in a large kettle about 45 minutes or until chicken is tender. Remove chicken from broth; cool, remove meat from bones, and dice. Strain broth; add enough water to make 2 cups.
    Sauté chopped onion and curry powder in butter until lightly browned. Stir in broth, chicken, half-and-half, and corn. Heat just to simmering and serve at once. Yield: 6 servings.

JAMBALAYA FOR A CROWD

12½ pounds fryer chickens, cut into
    serving-size pieces
    Salad oil
  3 pounds chopped onion
  1 pod garlic, minced
  1 bunch green onion, chopped
  1 large green pepper, chopped
    Water (2 parts water to 1 part
    rice)
    Salt and pepper to taste
    Worcestershire sauce (optional)
  6 pounds regular, uncooked rice

Fry chicken in small amount of salad oil.
Drain almost all the oil from cooking pot.
Add onion, garlic, green onion, and green
pepper; cook until lightly browned. Add
water and boil for 15 minutes. Add salt,
pepper, and Worcestershire sauce. Stir in
rice. Stir mixture once; cover pot tightly
and let mixture cook until all water has
been absorbed and rice is tender. Yield:
25 servings.

BRUNSWICK STEW

  3 (4- to 5-pound) hens
  2 pounds calf liver
12 large onions, finely chopped
  5 pounds potatoes, diced
  2 gallons canned tomatoes
  2 gallons canned corn
  1 gallon chicken stock
  2 quarts milk
  2 pounds butter
  2 (12-ounce) bottles chili sauce
    Worcestershire sauce
    Hot sauce
    Salt and pepper

Boil hens for several hours; save stock.
Remove meat from bones, and cut it into
small pieces as for hash. Boil and grind
liver. Combine onions, potatoes, and
meat in a large pot (preferably iron). Add
tomatoes, corn, chicken stock, milk, and
butter. Cook slowly, and after stew
begins to simmer, stir constantly until it
thickens well. Season liberally with chili
sauce, Worcestershire, hot sauce, salt,
and pepper. Yield: 80 servings.

CHICKEN STEW

    Salt and pepper
  1 (3- to 4-pound) stewing chicken, cut
    up
  ½ cup salad oil
  3 tablespoons all-purpose flour
  2 cups chopped onion
  ½ cup chopped celery
  ½ cup chopped green pepper
  2 cups water
  1 (4-ounce) can mushrooms
  ¼ cup chopped onion tops or
    shallots
  2 tablespoons chopped parsley
    Cooked rice

Salt and pepper chicken pieces; brown
quickly in hot oil. Remove chicken and
drain on absorbent paper. Add flour to oil
and stir until brown. Add onion, celery,
and green pepper; cook slowly until
tender. Return chicken to pan. Add water
and mushrooms. Cover and simmer for
2½ to 3 hours. Add onion tops about 10
minutes before chicken is done. Add
parsley 5 minutes before removing from
heat. Serve with cooked rice. Yield: 8
servings.

Index

Index